D1526067

JUMPSTART YOUR MACHINE LEARNING JOURNEY: LEARN EFFORTLESSLY, EVEN WITH NO PRIOR EXPERIENCE

ACCELERATE YOUR CAREER IN DATA SCIENCE AND ARTIFICIAL INTELLIGENCE WITH MACHINE LEARNING

SMART LEARNING SOLUTIONS

CONTENTS

INTRODUCTION

We find ourselves in the future we once dreamed of, and at the heart of this transformation are the remarkable advancements in Artificial Intelligence (AI) and Machine Learning (ML). This revolution has touched every aspect of our lives, from the devices we carry to the medical care we receive.

It's reshaping how we work and live and how we connect. Let's peek into how people perceive AI and ML.

HOW PEOPLE PERCEIVE AI AND ML

Angela often finds the perceived intricacies of machine learning daunting. She strongly desires to venture into this realm but believes that it will be difficult to grasp. The abundance of technical terminology alone can be pretty overwhelming for her.

On the other hand, John often grapples with uncertainty when embarking on his journey into machine learning. Despite encountering numerous online articles, the lack of a clear and comprehensive guide leaves him feeling adrift and unsure about where and how to start.

Jacob needs help comprehending the jargon and technical terminology of machine learning. He's searching for a guide to simplify these intricate complexities into easily under-standable and straightforward explanations.

Meanwhile, Joshua often encounters difficulty when attempting to put theoretical concepts into practice within real-life situations. He yearns for examples and case studies that can aid him in absorbing the lessons more effectively.

Lastly, Michelle experiences a sense of being left behind as the fields of AI and ML rapidly advance. The fear of missing out (FOMO) on these developments is causing her to feel anxious and unsettled.

If you can see yourself in any of these men and women, don't worry. You took a proactive step when you bought this book. You realize that you need help. You want to understand AI and ML, and I can empathize with you. I know you and your needs.

WHAT YOU CAN GAIN FROM READING THIS BOOK

As you read this book, I'll guide you through a distinctive framework designed to demystify and help you apply Machine Learning. Through relatable examples, interactive exercises, real-world use cases, and simplified explanations, you'll uncover the magic of ML at your own pace.

This book differs from the ones you've read because of its dedication to simplicity, approachability, and real-world relevance. Its approach is for beginners in a landscape where resources can often be complex or abstract, offering a comprehensive yet easily digestible introduction to Machine Learning.

As you progress, you'll build a strong ML foundation, arming yourself with the know-how and practical skills to harness ML's potential in your professional journey. With these tools, you'll confidently embrace opportunities in this field, ensuring that you're well-prepared to navigate the future shaped by AI advancements.

ABOUT THE AUTHOR

I established Smart Learning Solutions with the heartfelt goal of assisting newcomers in their journey into Artificial Intelligence learning, drawing from my own experiences on a similar path. With a quarter-century of experience in the same field, I recognize the constant evolution that demands us to enhance our skills and to continually remain meaningful.

I aim to offer guidance and answers to those who, like me, are navigating the dynamic world of AI and Machine Learning, providing a helping hand in this transformative domain.

WHAT YOU CAN LEARN FROM EACH CHAPTER

Chapter 1: Setting the Stage: Introduction to Artificial Intelligence and Machine Learning

In Chapter 1, you'll grasp the fundamental concepts of AI and ML and recognize their significance in our modern reality. You can gain a sturdy base to comprehend the essence of AI and ML and their profound importance in our lives today.

Chapter 2: Invisible Hands: Machine Learning in Our Daily Lives

Chapter 2 helps you absorb the impact of ML through relatable real-world instances. You'll learn the subtle ways in which ML intertwines with our daily experiences, often escaping our awareness.

Chapter 3: Getting Technical: Key Concepts and Terminologies

In Chapter 3, you learn the fundamental ML concepts and terminology. I simplified the complex language to ensure that ML concepts become approachable and understandable for you.

Chapter 4: From Theory to Practice: Machine Learning Algorithms

Chapter 4 helps you gain profound insights into diverse ML algorithms and how they are applied. We delve deep into the heart of ML and its algorithms and provide clear, relatable explanations of their purposes and applications.

Chapter 5: Data: The Fuel of Machine Learning

In Chapter 5, you'll understand the pivotal significance of data in ML and learning methods to prepare data effectively. You learn data's crucial role in ML and illustrate methods to ready it for fruitful and effective ML endeavors.

Chapter 6: Hands-On Machine Learning: Building Your First Model

Chapter 6 helps you grasp a step-by-step roadmap for putting into practice and refining an ML model. We embark on your inaugural hands-on ML project, reinforcing the theoretical insights you've acquired on your journey.

Chapter 7: Stepping Up the Ladder: Career Opportunities

In Chapter 7, you gain a clear view of potential career paths within ML and receive advice on the essential skills needed. You'll learn a wide array of career prospects available in the dynamic world of ML. Moreover, I also offer practical pointers on how to embark on these paths.

Chapter 8: Beyond the Horizon: Future Trends and Developments

Chapter 8 helps you understand the outlook of ML's future and recognize the ongoing need for learning. You'll get a glimpse into the upcoming trends in ML. I hope to motivate you to embrace a continuous learning mindset to stay informed and relevant in this ever-evolving field.

THIS BOOK IS RIGHT FOR YOU

I wrote the book for a varied range of potential readers. You can be a student or a new member of the workforce. You may even be a mid-career professional who wants to enhance your skills or change career paths. Even if you're just plain curious, this book is for you.

You're the reason I wrote this book. I perceive you as someone who can master AI and ML. You're the right fit to read and understand machine learning effortlessly, even if you are inexperienced. We'll start with a basic introduction first.

SETTING THE STAGE: INTRODUCTION TO ARTIFICIAL INTELLIGENCE AND MACHINE LEARNING

Have you ever wondered how Netflix suggestions work? The Netflix Recommendation Engine (NRE) employs advanced machine learning techniques like reinforcement learning, matrix factorization, and other algorithmic approaches to organize and prioritize content recommendations effectively.

But before discussing advanced techniques, let's tackle the basics first.

WHAT IS ARTIFICIAL INTELLIGENCE?

Artificial Intelligence (AI) is a diverse field aiming to create intelligent machines that can perform some tasks that humans do. The spotlight on deep learning and machine learning drives transformative changes in technology.

AI empowers machines to replicate human cognitive abilities, from autonomous vehicles to creative tools like ChatGPT and Google's Bard. Its integration into daily life is increasing, prompting significant investments across industries. AI's impact shapes various aspects of our world, with businesses dedicating resources to harness its potential.

How Does Artificial Intelligence Work?

Companies are eager to showcase their use of AI, but often what they label as AI is just a part of it, like machine learning. Specific hardware and software tools are required to create and train machine learning algorithms for AI applications. Popular programming languages for AI development include Julia, C++, Java, R, and Python.

AI systems process labeled training data to identify trends and patterns, making them capable of predicting future situations. Examples include chatbots learning realistic conversations and image recognition tools identifying objects in images, with new AI techniques producing lifelike creative content.

AI programming revolves around specific cognitive skills:

- **Learning:** This part of AI programming is about gathering data and creating rules (called algorithms) to transform the data into useful information. These algorithms provide successive instructions to computers on how to finish a specific task.

- **Reasoning:** In AI programming, reason involves selecting the best algorithm to achieve a desired outcome.
- **Self-correction:** This facet of AI programming focuses on constantly refining algorithms to ensure that they deliver the most accurate and precise results.
- **Creativity:** AI's creative side employs various techniques like statistical methods, rule-based systems, and neural networks to generate innovative ideas, text, and fresh images.

AI involves training machines to think like humans, which allows them to understand, predict, and even create things. It's an exciting field that is changing how technology works, and it's impacting our lives in numerous ways.

What Is the Relevance of Artificial Intelligence?

AI's significance lies in its transformative potential for reshaping our lives, jobs, and leisure. It effectively handles tasks like customer service, fraud detection, and quality assurance in business. AI excels in intricate and repetitive tasks, outperforming humans in fields such as legal document analysis. Its capability to process vast datasets offers valuable operational insights.

Generative AI tools are poised to revolutionize education, marketing, and product design. AI's progress enhances efficiency and creates new business opportunities, as exemplified by Uber's success in connecting passengers through AI.

Leading companies like Alphabet, Apple, Microsoft, and Meta leverage AI for a competitive edge, and Google's subsidiary, Waymo, uses AI in self-driving cars and innovative Google Brain projects. AI is reshaping businesses, unlocking new possibilities, and driving significant technological advancements in today's fast-paced world.

How Did Artificial Intelligence Begin?

The "thinking machine" concept has roots in ancient Greece, but it gained momentum with the emergence of electronic computing. Several key moments stand out in the evolution of artificial intelligence:

- **1950:** Alan Turing, known for his World War II accomplishments in breaking the ENIGMA code, published "Computing Machinery and Intelligence." In this paper, he addressed whether machines are capable of thinking. Moreover, he introduced the Turing Test to ascertain the computer's capability to show human-like intelligence. However, the significance of the Turing Test is still being debated.
- **1956:** John McCarthy introduced "artificial intelligence" at the first Dartmouth College AI conference. The same year, Herbert Simon, J.C. Shaw, and Allen Newell created the first operational

AI software program: Logic Theorist, a program that proved theorems using symbolic logic.

- **1967:** Frank Rosenblatt designed a neural-network-based computer that learns through experimentation: the Mark 1 Perceptron. Marvin Minsky and Seymour Papert's book *Perceptrons* became a critical work on neural networks but generated some debate against further neural network research for a period of time.

- **The 1980s:** Backpropagation algorithm in neural networks gained extensive use in AI applications.

- **1997:** Deep Blue, an IBM creation, defeated Garry Kasparov, a chess champion, and marked AI's victory over human expertise.

- **2011:** IBM's Watson surpasses human champions Ken Jennings and Brad Rutter in the game show *Jeopardy!*, showcasing AI's prowess in answering complex questions.

- **2015:** Baidu's Minwa supercomputer achieved significant accuracy in detecting and classifying images. A deep neural network, known as convolutional, powered it. Moreover, this supercomputer surpassed human capabilities.

- **2016:** DeepMind's AlphaGo program, backed by deep neural networks, defeats world Go champion Lee Sodol in a significant five-game match. It's notable due to the immense complexity of the game. Google later acquired DeepMind.

- **2023:** A significant shift occurs with the rise of large language models like ChatGPT, dramatically enhancing AI's capabilities and potential business value. These advanced AI models are trainable on massive amounts of unlabeled, raw data, revolutionizing the field.

The journey of AI has seen numerous breakthroughs, from machines trying to think like humans to beating humans at intricate games and tasks. Each step has paved the way for AI to affect several aspects of our lives and to open doors to new possibilities. Today, there are several current types of AI.

What Are the Classifications of AI?

AI applications are categorized into three types, highlighting their evolution. AI is a tool that humans design that is not meant to replace them. It's currently programmed software that is useful for specific tasks.

As AI advances, a comprehensive framework is needed to address legal, ethical, and moral concerns surrounding its use. The potential emergence of more advanced AI types with human-like traits poses regulatory challenges for developed societies. Understanding these categories is crucial for shaping the future of AI.

Narrow Artificial Intelligence

Narrow Artificial Intelligence (Narrow AI) is the prevailing form of AI today, showcasing its influence across mobile applications, the internet, and large-scale data analysis. The word "narrow" signifies that this type of AI is purpose-built for specific tasks, excelling in its focused capabilities.

This specific orientation, limited to its designated tasks and lacking versatility, earns it the label of "weak" AI. This specialization allows for fine-tuning and optimization of its performance, honing its intelligence in a specific domain.

The name "narrow" is fitting due to several reasons:

- **Complex Computer Program:** Narrow AI is a sophisticated computer program tailored to solve a specific problem. Its structure and function align closely with this objective.
- **Adaptation to Current Standards and Tools:** AI enhances specific operations and yields significant returns in the business landscape. The technology's present state is conducive to catering to these requirements, prioritizing task-oriented solutions.

The efficiency, speed, and precision of narrow AI surpass human capabilities, making it a preferred solution for many corporations. It seamlessly handles repetitive tasks, often involving vast datasets, known as "big data." With the prevalence of data collection, companies can harness this infor-mation to train AI and draw valuable insights.

Examples of Narrow AI Applications

- **Recommendation Systems:** Platforms like Netflix, YouTube, and Twitter employ narrow AI to tailor recommendations based on user preferences, enhancing their experience.
- **Spam Filtering:** Narrow AI equipped with natural language processing effectively manages and filters spam emails, ensuring inboxes remain clutter-free.
- **Expert Systems:** Narrow AI has the potential to form the basis of expert systems, which could represent the future of AI. These systems have smaller, narrow AI components akin to human intelligence's diverse abilities. For instance, IBM Watson incorporates natural language processing and cognitive aspects.

As AI evolves, the role of narrow AI remains pivotal, solving specific challenges and laying the foundation for more advanced forms of AI in the future.

General Artificial Intelligence

General Artificial Intelligence (general AI), which also goes by the name strong AI or artificial general intelligence (AGI), aims to emulate human thinking and functioning across a wide range of abilities.

Unlike narrow AI designed for specific tasks, general AI can handle tasks like vision, language comprehension, critical thinking, and holistic reasoning. It requires unsupervised learning for adaptability and breadth, distinguishing it from guided learning in narrow AI.

However, achieving general AI is challenging due to the intricacy of human intelligence. Despite advancements in neural networks, understanding "intelligence" and defining "consciousness"–crucial for AGI–remain significant obstacles.

Obstacles of General Artificial Intelligence

The journey towards general AI faces various obstacles, including:

- **Transfer Learning:** A vital aspect of human cognition is transferring knowledge gained in one domain to another. Recent advances in neural networks have been promising. For an accomplished AGI, robust transfer learning capabilities are crucial, ensuring that it can apply existing knowledge to new situations without retraining.
- **Common Sense and Collaboration:** Human intelligence relies on common sense and collaboration with fellow humans. However, existing algorithms need this capacity. Developing a true general AI involves instilling these

characteristics, enabling it to collaborate with other machines and humans.

- **Understanding Consciousness and the Mind:** Consciousness is fundamental to human experience and plays a central role in recognizing intelligence. Furthermore, the intricacies of the human mind remain unsolved. Both of these aspects pose significant challenges in achieving general artificial intelligence.

General Artificial Intelligence Examples

- **Chatbots**

Chatbots use Natural Language Processing (NLP) to analyze human conversations and create replies. In the context of general intelligence, a system would independently formulate answers without relying on the opinions of others. Moreover, it would comprehend the nuanced meanings of its responses, such as understanding the significance of concepts like walls and their associations with locations like Mexico.

- **Autonomous Vehicles**

With years of anticipation, autonomous vehicles have captured our imaginations with their potential. Companies like Tesla, Uber, and Waymo have been at the front line of this technological development. They've achieved Level 4 automation, enabling cars to operate without human input under specific conditions.

The ultimate goal, Level 5 automation, envisions vehicles acting intuitively without human intervention, regardless of the situation. However, reaching this level is highly challenging, requiring an advanced form of AI (AGI) to handle the myriad scenarios that could arise during a journey.

Generally, AI represents the pinnacle of AI development, with capabilities mirroring human intelligence. While it presents remarkable potential, its realization involves surmounting intricate obstacles crucial to its eventual success.

- **Artificial Super Intelligence**

Artificial Super Intelligence (ASI) signifies AI surpassing human cognitive abilities and is a speculative concept in AI development. Envisioned scenarios suggest that ASI could result from an "Intelligence Explosion" propelled by exponential AI algorithm advancement.

This explosion involves recursive self-improvement, where an AI system learns from its knowledge to enhance intelligence rapidly. Starting from average human intelligence, the AI progresses to genius levels, compounding its capabilities with each iteration. Despite its theoretical potential, achieving or controlling ASI remains in science fiction.

However, before focusing on Super AI, it's vital to learn about an AI subset at the forefront of the technologies we use today—Machine Learning.

MACHINE LEARNING: A SUBGROUP OF AI

Machine learning powers several technologies that we deal with every day. It's the technology at the core of Netflix recommendations, language translation apps, predictive text, content arrangement in your social media feeds, and chatbots. It also empowers self-driving vehicles and machines capable of diagnosing medical conditions through image analysis.

Companies implementing AI systems today will likely utilize machine learning extensively. These terms are frequently interchangeable; thus, they need clarification. Machine learning is a specialized feature of AI. It empowers computers to learn from data without requiring explicit programming instructions. In simpler terms, it allows computers to understand and improve independently.

What Is Machine Learning?

Machine learning is a crucial artificial intelligence component that allows computers to understand and decide without explicit programming. It enables computers to extract insights from data, identify patterns, and make informed choices, reducing the need for extensive human intervention.

As a subset of AI, machine learning aims to replicate human-like behavior and decision-making by facilitating independent learning through automated processes. It involves providing machines with quality data and employing diverse algorithms to create adaptable machine-learning models.

Unlike traditional programming, where predefined rules dictate output, machine learning involves machines constructing their programs based on input data and corresponding results during a learning phase.

How Machine Learning Came About

The journey of machine learning began with the introduction of the first neural network model by Walter Pitts and Warren McCulloch in 1943, shaping the foundation of AI development. Key milestones include Donald Hebb's theories linking behavior with neural networks in 1949 and Alan Turing's Turing Test in 1950 to evaluate computer intelligence.

Advancements followed, such as Arthur Samuel's computer learning program for checkers in 1952 and Frank Rosenblatt's perceptron in 1957. Succeeding decades produced innovations, such as:

- The transformative GPT-3 language model by OpenAI
- Breakthroughs in deep learning
- Data-driven machine learning
- Explanation based learning
- The emergence of deep neural networks

These milestones collectively showcase the impressive evolution of machine learning over the years. As Machine Learning becomes part of human innovation, let's understand how its algorithm works.

How Machine Learning Algorithms Works

Machine learning involves computers analyzing data to discover patterns, enabling more accurate predictions on new data sets—a process akin to human understanding. Just as humans draw on past experiences to make decisions, machine learning models learn from historical data to autonomously make predictions—a fundamental aspect of AI.

An illustrative example is the dinosaur game in Google Chrome, which an AI could learn to play based on trial and error, adapting decisions based on conditions. Analogous to recognizing patterns in sequences, machine learning models learn from collected data to enhance predictions.

Central to machine learning are mathematical functions that underlie algorithms, forming the basis of the learning process, which is deeply rooted in mathematics. As humans learn from experiences to make better choices, machine learning uses mathematical principles to enhance predictions and decisions.

Types of Machine Learning

In the realm of machine learning, various methods of AI systems learn from data. These methods are categorized based on the type of data involved (labeled or unlabeled) and the desired outcomes. There are four broad primary machine learning types: supervised, unsupervised, semi-supervised, and reinforcement learning.

Supervised Learning

Managed learning is akin to a teacher-student dynamic. A data scientist is a teacher instructing the AI system using predefined rules and labeled datasets. These datasets contain input data paired with expected output results. The AI system needs explicit guidance on what to identify in the input data.

Supervised learning is about learning from examples. These examples form the training data. Once a machine learning model can use this data, it's tested with new data to gauge its accuracy. Supervised learning further splits into regression and classification tasks.

Unsupervised Learning

Unsupervised learning operates like an observer. In this approach, the AI system learns by identifying patterns in input data without corresponding output data. Unlike supervised learning, there's no specific guidance; the system needs a lot of unlabeled data to identify patterns and to learn from them.

Unsupervised learning can serve as a standalone goal, like revealing hidden patterns in data or learning features. It involves clustering and association problems.

Semi-Supervised Learning

Semi-supervised learning blends aspects of both supervised and unsupervised methods. Here, the AI system receives initial training to gain a general understanding.

Unlike supervised learning, the AI system must discern patterns independently from the data. Semi-supervised education proves helpful when labeled data is scarce or costly, but an accurate model is still desirable.

Reinforcement Learning

Reinforcement learning takes an interactive approach. In this technique, an AI system learns within a dynamic environment. A programmer employs a system of rewards and penalties to guide the AI's learning process.

The AI system learns by experimentation, getting feedback from its actions. In simple terms, AI faces a game scenario where it strives to maximize rewards. While the programmer sets the rules, the AI must determine the optimal strategy through repeated attempts, learning, and improvement.

These machine learning methods provide AI systems with distinct ways to learn, adapting to different situations and environments, much like how we learn from teachers, observations, partial knowledge, or interactive experiences.

But why should we learn about Machine Language?

WHY STUDY MACHINE LANGUAGE

Machine Learning has evolved into a powerful technology that major companies like Walmart and Uber utilize for content curation, fraud detection, and product recommendations.

Its integration into daily services and strong career prospects stem from its widespread application in domains like email, mobile apps, and marketing. Acquiring machine learning skills is valuable for those pursuing a dynamic and high-demand career path.

Promising Career Path in Machine Learning

Machine learning offers promising career opportunities as AI-driven services experience substantial growth and revenue, with industries actively seeking skilled professionals to develop innovative solutions in fields like cyber-security and medicine.

Large companies are hiring ML engineers to drive business intelligence, demonstrated by instances like Netflix offering rewards for algorithm enhancement. As demand rises, aspiring IT professionals have a favorable chance to enter the field and contribute to its ongoing advancement.

Attractive Earnings for Machine Learning Engineers

Machine learning engineers receive handsome rewards. On average, they earn around $142,000 a year, with experienced professionals making up to $195,752, according to SimplyHired.com. This promising salary range puts machine learning engineers in a league comparable to top athletes, underlining the lucrative nature of this career.

Thriving Job Market in Machine Learning

Machine learning engineers enjoy a booming job market. Leading tech companies are actively recruiting individuals with the expertise to develop impactful machine learning algorithms. The demand for these specialized professionals is evident from the significant increase in job postings, surpassing the number of job searches.

Cities like Bangalore, India alone require thousands of machine learning engineers. The job market is exceptionally dynamic, making it a golden era for those pursuing a career in machine learning.

Shortage of Machine Learning Skills Lamented by CIOs

The skills gap in machine learning concerns organizations, hindering their efforts for digital transformation. CIOs need help finding the right talent because of the need for more available experts.

A Gartner report highlights the scarcity of machine learning skills, particularly in locations like New York (ProjectPro, 2023). The demand for skilled professionals is higher than its current supply. This scarcity presents a unique opportunity for aspiring machine learning engineers to fill this void and to excel in their careers.

Machine Learning and Data Science Synergy

Machine learning closely relates to data science. Pursuing a career in machine learning equips individuals with a dual role as machine learning engineers and data scientists.

Proficiency in both domains makes individuals highly sought-after by employers. This versatility allows professionals to analyze vast amounts of data, extract insights, and apply them to train machine learning models.

Cooperation between data scientists and machine learning engineers is familiar, further emphasizing the value of this combined skill set. Becoming adept in data science and machine learning enhances career prospects, aligning with the growing importance of data-driven decision-making.

Embarking on a journey in machine learning promises a dynamic and rewarding career driven by demand, innovation, and the convergence of cutting-edge technology. We'll discuss more jobs in machine learning in Chapter 7.

In summary, machine learning is a vital component of today's technology landscape, enabling computers to learn autonomously from data, similar to human learning. It encompasses various methods, such as supervised, unsupervised, semi-supervised, and reinforcement learning, tailored to diverse learning scenarios.

Since its inception with neural networks in 1943, machine learning has achieved significant milestones. Artificial intelligence uses these advancements to create intelligent machines capable of human-like tasks. These machines affect industries from autonomous vehicles to creative tools like ChatGPT.

AI's evolution gears toward general AI, though challenges like common sense understanding persist. The concept of artificial superintelligence (ASI) envisions AI surpassing human cognitive abilities.

Machine learning, a subset of AI, uses statistical techniques to navigate data, offering promising career prospects and ample opportunities, especially when combined with data science expertise.

Collaboration between data scientists and machine learning engineers is common, enhancing the value of this dual skill set. A career in machine learning promises innovation and high demand, making it a dynamic and rewarding field to explore.

Now that you know the basics of Artificial Intelligence and Machine Learning, we'll discuss their invisible influence in our daily lives next.

INVISIBLE HANDS: MACHINE LEARNING IN OUR DAILY LIVES

D id you know that Machine Learning powers our daily lives, from online shopping recommendations to traffic predictions on your commute?

Some assert that we are on the brink of experiencing a new phase akin to an industrial revolution propelled by AI advancements. While the earlier Industrial Revolution leveraged physical and mechanical prowess, this emerging revolution centers around mental and cognitive capabilities.

Envision a future where computers not only supplant physical tasks but also undertake mental tasks. The transition is already in motion, but how will it unfold?

Just as machines mechanized physical tasks during the Industrial Revolution, AI is poised to handle mental tasks. Let's look at how Machine Learning affects healthcare, finance, transportation, and other sectors.

MACHINE LEARNING IN HEALTHCARE

Machine learning is revolutionizing healthcare by harnessing the power of data and algorithms to transform how medical professionals diagnose, treat, and predict health conditions.

This cutting-edge technology enables personalized care, predictive analytics, and faster decision-making, ushering in a new era of precision medicine and improved patient outcomes.

Before we delve deeper into how healthcare benefits from machine learning, let's discuss the various types of AI trailblazing the industry.

Types of AI Revolutionizing Healthcare

Artificial intelligence is transforming healthcare, with machine learning playing a pivotal role. Different forms of AI reshape the health sector by enhancing medical systems, uncovering patterns in extensive data, and creating intelligent medical tools.

- **Machine learning** is a digital diagnostic assistant analyzing clinical data to identify health trends and expedite diagnoses.
- **Natural Language Processing (NLP)** acts as a language expert, extracting patient information from doctors' notes for seamless care.

- **Physical robots** assist surgeons, ensuring precision and reducing complications.
- **Robotic Process Automation (RPA)** automates tasks, freeing up medical professionals for more impactful work.

Together, these AI elements revolutionize patient care and amplify healthcare's potential. Now that you know the various aspects at play in revolutionizing the healthcare industry, it's good to know the vital role that machine learning plays.

Machine Learning's Vital Role in Healthcare

In healthcare, machine learning is a superhero that navigates through vast electronic health records to uncover patterns and insights invisible to human eyes.

This technology revolutionizes healthcare by enabling a predictive technique to precision medicine, seamless care delivery, and improved processes. It assists with managing medical bills, guiding clinical decisions, and creating practice guidelines.

Real-world applications include predicting harmful effects in cancer patients undergoing therapy. Machine learning enables medical data to reveal intricate patterns autonomously, aiding primary care in digital health records.

With nearly 80% of healthcare data remaining unstructured, machine learning is a code-breaker, utilizing artificial intelligence and natural language processing to transform complex language into valuable insights.

In partnership with deep learning, it deciphers patient records and uncovers healthcare's hidden treasures, enhancing care and illuminating a healthier future.

Empowering Healthcare: The Benefits of Machine Learning

Machine learning is a transformative force in healthcare, offering numerous benefits. Wearable tech combined with machine learning swiftly gathers real-time patient data, aided by the integration of AI into medical devices. Machine learning and deep learning models expedite drug discovery because they predict drug molecules accurately.

Machine learning algorithms enhance efficiency by sorting through electronic health records, automating tasks, and freeing healthcare professionals' time. They ensure personalized patient care because machine learning analyzes extensive data sets to create tailored treatments and to predict patient responses to specific drugs.

Machine learning accelerates discoveries, streamlines processes, and revolutionizes healthcare, promising a brighter future for the field. Let's look at some real-world machine learning applications in revolutionizing the industry.

Revolutionizing Healthcare With Machine Learning: Real-World Applications

Machine learning revolutionizes healthcare with diverse applications that reshape patient care and outcomes. It predicts disease outbreaks, uncovers hidden trends, and enhances disease management.

Visualizing biomedical data reveals intricate RNA sequences, protein structures, and genomics details. Machine learning aids in accurate diagnoses by identifying symptom patterns for early disease detection. It seamlessly transfers up-to-date patient records among medical professionals, fostering holistic care coordination.

AI-assisted surgery enhances precision, aids in complex tasks, and provides clearer visuals. Personalized patient-centric decisions using multi-modal data help achieve tailored treatments.

Machine learning optimizes medical research by refining participant selection and analyzing trial results. It also pioneers drug development by identifying potential pathways for innovative medications. Machine learning is shaping a future of precise, proactive care and groundbreaking innovation in healthcare.

Machine Learning Examples in Healthcare

Machine learning is driving transformative changes in healthcare, offering remarkable examples that showcase its potential. Let's look at how a few companies use the technology.

Microsoft's Impact on Healthcare Through Machine Learning

Founded in 1975, Microsoft has been a trailblazer in the technology industry. Located in Redmond, Washington, the company has led innovation for decades. Through Project InnerEye, Microsoft transforms healthcare by combining computer vision and machine learning to interpret intricate 3D radiological images.

The objective is to accurately differentiate between tumors and healthy structures, aiding in radiotherapy and surgical planning. This initiative empowers medical professionals with AI-guided decision-making, enhancing precision and personalized treatments.

Microsoft envisions a future where healthcare is tailor-fit to individual requirements, ushering in a new era of medical advancement.

Tempus: Pioneering Cancer Research Through Machine Learning

Established in Chicago, Illinois in 2015, Tempus is reshaping healthcare with innovation. With a focus on cancer research, Tempus employs machine learning to gather extensive medical data, aiming to revolutionize personalized treatments for cancer patients.

Their data repository is immense, and AI-driven algorithms enable Tempus to make breakthroughs in areas like genomic profiling, clinical trial matching, diagnostic biomarking, and academic research. Tempus offers hope to cancer patients by utilizing machine learning to create a future of personalized and effective treatments.

PathAI: Advancing Healthcare With Machine Learning

Founded in Boston, Massachusetts in 2016, PathAI has become a prominent force in healthcare. Using cutting-edge machine learning, they empower pathologists to make quicker and more accurate diagnoses, revolutionizing healthcare.

Beyond diagnostics, their AI tools streamline patient information, sample processing, and tasks crucial for clinical trials and drug development. PathAI's strong network across biopharma groups, labs, and clinicians positions them to deliver effective treatments and advancements, illuminating a promising future for patients. By combining machine learning with medical expertise, PathAI is driving progress in diagnostics and treatment.

Beta Bionics: Transforming Diabetes Care through Machine Learning

Founded in 2015 in Boston, Massachusetts, Beta Bionics is a pioneering force in healthcare innovation. Their objective is to enhance the lives of individuals with diabetes, achieved through their groundbreaking creation, the iLet.

This wearable bionic "pancreas," empowered by machine learning, continuously tracks blood sugar levels in patients with Type 1 diabetes. The iLet offers patients freedom from constant blood sugar tracking, enabling less burdensome and more stress-free diabetes management.

Beta Bionics is a symbol of relief for diabetes patients, using machine learning and wearable technology to simplify and enhance diabetes management.

Pfizer: Elevating Immuno-Oncology Research with Machine Learning

Pfizer, a longstanding pillar in healthcare since its establishment in 1848 in New York City, is using the power of machine learning to promote immuno-oncology research. Collaborating with IBM's Watson AI technology, Pfizer aims to unlock the potential of the body's immune system to combat cancer.

This partnership accelerates the analysis of extensive patient data, transforming it into actionable insights for more effective cancer treatments. By leveraging machine learning, Pfizer is leading the charge in reshaping cancer care, offering hope and transformative possibilities for patients and their families.

Aside from machine learning use cases in healthcare, it's also at the forefront of revolutionizing the finance industry.

MACHINE LEARNING IN FINANCE

Machine learning is a game-changer in finance, revolutionizing how financial companies operate and make decisions. With its ability to enhance risk management, automate tasks, and analyze vast amounts of data, machine learning is transforming the financial sector, leading to greater efficiency and precision.

Machine Learning's Game-Changing Role in Finance

Machine learning is revolutionizing the landscape of financial security, enhancing cybersecurity measures and transforming various aspects of the finance industry. Automated investment advisors powered by machine learning provide early insights into market changes, transforming investment banking practices. Automation streamlines tasks, improves customer experiences, and reduces costs.

Machine learning serves as a vigilant guardian against transactional fraud by analyzing data to uncover hidden threats, minimizing recovery costs due to fraud. It revolutionizes risk management by comprehensively assessing risk through data analysis, guiding smarter decisions, and predicting potential defaulting customers.

In algorithmic trading, machine learning brings accuracy and responsiveness to market conditions. Robo-advisors driven by machine learning offer personalized financial advice, catering to individuals and small businesses.

Machine learning processes extensive financial data, extracting insights from market trends to customer behavior. It informs data-driven decisions, scrutinizing structured and unstructured data for risk assessment and customer insights.

Intelligent chatbots enhance customer service by responding to queries and offering personalized information. Machine learning predicts customer retention, tailoring offers to ensure loyalty. Moreover, machine learning crafts effective marketing strategies by analyzing past behaviors and responses, achieving marketing precision and excellence.

Unleashing Machine Learning's Benefits in Finance

Machine learning is a transformative force in finance, offering error-free precision by minimizing human errors and ensuring accurate data. Its efficiency accelerates processes, providing real-time solutions for quick and precise decision-making. The initial investment in machine learning yields long-term rewards as AI and ML evolve, becoming more competent and cost-effective.

Machine learning eases the workload burden by automating tedious tasks, freeing human effort, and enhancing overall efficiency. Notably, machine learning's unbiased nature ensures fairness in decision-making, offering transparent and impartial data-driven judgments crucial in the finance industry.

Machine Learning's Applications in Financial Markets

Machine learning is revolutionizing corporate finance by automating tasks like data entry and financial monitoring, freeing up employees for higher-level jobs. It enhances customer relations through automation, improving customer engagement and acquisition.

Data from Internet of Things (IoT) devices leads to personalized marketing and better customer service, increasing satisfaction and retention. Machine learning also aids in predicting stock markets. Moreover, it assesses loan applications and credit scores for online lending, providing real-time recommendations.

Machine learning analyzes historical data to assess risks and assist in investment decisions. It extracts insights from unstructured data, giving a competitive edge through better data-driven decisions.

Machine learning detects issues and automates resolutions in trade settlements, eliminating errors and delays. It also refines asset valuation and management, ensuring accurate decisions. Machine learning is reshaping finance from automation to prediction, ushering in a new era of data-driven precision.

Let's look at some startups changing the financial landscape.

Revolutionary Startups Changing the Finance Landscape

In the dynamic landscape of finance, revolutionary startups are sparking transformation. These startups herald a new era of efficiency, inclusivity, and user-centric financial services. Let's discuss some of these companies.

Detecting Fraud with Signifyd

Signifyd leads the pack in AI-driven startups, straddling banking and e-commerce. It's a fraud identification solution that deploys deep learning to authenticate customers and evaluate payment intent based on past behaviors and transactions.

Streamlining with HyperScience

HyperScience redefines productivity with AI and machine learning. Its Intelligent Document Processing technology transforms handwritten invoices into precise data, erasing errors and boosting efficiency.

Auditing Made Smart by AppZen

AppZen transforms auditing through machine learning. Armed with Natural Language Processing and advanced computer vision, this platform examines contracts and invoices for errors, fraud, and spending patterns.

Smart Credit Scoring by Zest

Zest reshapes credit scoring using advanced credit modeling. This ML-powered solution assesses potential risks and empowers lenders with data-driven insights, aligning with the principles of open finance.

Futuristic Wealth Management via FutureAdvisor

FutureAdvisor doesn't just gather data; it predicts using analytics. This platform employs predictive analytics to guide investment decisions and wealth management strategies, all while optimizing taxation prospects.

Cleo: Your Smart Financial Buddy

Startups aren't just for banks—Cleo is an AI-powered budgeting app. It studies your spending habits, suggests budgeting techniques, sets financial goals, and helps you achieve them. Cleo's user-friendly design makes finance management a breeze.

These startups are rewriting the finance rulebook. Their AI and machine learning prowess shape a new era of efficient and savvy finance management for businesses and individuals, from fraud detection to more competent auditing.

Machine learning doesn't only help revolutionize health-care and finance. It's also at the forefront of improving the transportation sector.

MACHINE LEARNING IN TRANSPORTATION

In the ever-evolving realm of transportation, machine learning emerges as a driving force of innovation. It revolutionizes navigating, optimizing routes and ensuring vehicle safety through artificial intelligence and data analysis. Its applications pave the way for a more innovative, efficient transportation landscape.

Revolutionizing Transportation: Machine Learning's Transformative Role

The transportation industry benefits immensely from the capabilities of machine learning. This technology is pivotal in transportation engineering, revolutionizing how we move. Machine learning becomes a driving force in transportation by predicting real-time traffic data, analyzing complex road information, and factoring in variables like accidents and weather.

Machine learning's power lies in fusing diverse data sources to enhance modern transportation and create more innovative city logistics. The ultimate goal is to optimize and streamline transportation systems by intelligently utilizing data from various avenues.

Machine Learning Benefits to Transportation

AI and ML transform the transportation sector by utilizing past data for informed decision-making. Their implementation enhances safety, reduces accidents, and allows crewless vehicles to improve road safety during nighttime accidents.

Self-driving vehicles with AI-driven systems predict traffic, monitor vehicle health, and detect medical emergencies, ensuring safety and prompt medical assistance.

For instance, AI can take over if a driver is too sleepy to drive. The vehicle's Smart Sensors can detect if the driver is having a heart attack. They can also alert medics in an emergency.

Automakers benefit from AI-driven technology through self-driving capabilities, predictive maintenance, and route optimization, opening new revenue streams while eliminating driver costs.

AI's capabilities extend to optimizing transportation scheduling, enabling operators to fine-tune public and private transportation services for improved efficiency. Applications like Google Maps leverage AI to provide real-time traffic updates and location-based predictions, aiding users in making well-informed travel decisions.

AI and ML are reshaping transportation by enhancing safety, efficiency, and predictive planning for a data-driven travel future.

Unlocking the Machine Learning Applications in Transportation

Machine Learning transforms transportation. Today, it can distinguish between several modes of transport. Moreover, it can enhance traffic management, navigation, delivery with drone taxis, self-driving cars, and vehicle control. The integration of Machine Learning and advanced data analytics enables real-time tracking of vehicles, improving navigation accuracy and providing voice-assisted guidance.

Machine Learning-powered apps empower users to remotely control vehicle settings, such as temperature, adding convenience to their experience. The reality of self-driving cars has been made possible through Machine Learning, allowing vehicles to navigate while having a human driver only for emergencies.

Drone taxis revolutionize logistics by enabling efficient parcel delivery and reducing travel time, emissions, and costs. Additionally, Machine Learning's impact on traffic management is substantial, optimizing routes and preventing congestion, resulting in smoother journeys for individuals and transportation companies.

This innovative approach reshapes transportation by providing an efficient and seamless way to interact with and navigate vehicles.

Machine learning is beneficial in changing the healthcare, finance, and transportation industries, and it is also boosting technological advancements in other sectors.

MACHINE LEARNING IN OTHER SECTORS

Machine Learning is reshaping industries by revolutionizing data handling and decision-making processes. ML empowers machines to learn and execute tasks without explicit programming through pattern recognition and logical predictions. Let's delve into the sectors where ML is making a profound impact.

Software Development

Understand the evolution of software development, where ML aids in diverse processes. Overcoming budget and timing concerns, ML analyzes data from past projects, offering accurate budget estimates. Developers no longer dictate decision rules; instead, learning algorithms detect essential patterns from data, even uncovering unforeseen details.

Transcription

Witness the transformation of the transcription industry through ML-powered speech-to-text software. Specialized Automated Speech Recognition (ASR) engines achieve remarkable accuracy when trained within specific domains.

ML-driven transcription solutions provide speed and precision, saving time and cost for tasks like converting emails and meeting minutes.

Retail and Customer Service

Amidst industry disruptions, ML emerged as a pivotal catalyst for change. Enabling supply chain reinvention, inventory management, and predictive user behavior analysis, ML reshapes retail and customer service. Chatbots enhance customer interaction, offering 24/7 AI-powered support, reducing costs, and elevating satisfaction.

Marketing

Use the prowess of ML in deciphering extensive data rapidly and effectively. Marketers leverage ML's ability to identify website activity patterns, enhance ad optimization, and predict user behavior. Personalized customer experiences lead to amplified profits, transforming the marketing landscape.

Manufacturing

A manufacturing revolution is happening, fueled by AI and ML. Enhancing production efficiency and cost-effectiveness, ML is pivotal in real-time error detection, supply chain visibility, and asset tracking. Harnessing ML's potential streamlines assembly and production processes, impacting bottom lines.

Cybersecurity

Understand ML's role as a cybersecurity cornerstone. ML-driven security systems analyze patterns to adapt to changing behavior and to thwart attacks. With improved threat detection and real-time response, cybersecurity teams can proactively safeguard organizations.

Agriculture

Learn about the technology's profound influence on agriculture. By integrating data into ML systems, real-time AI-driven recommendations empower farm management. Sensors and ML applications predict yields, assess crop quality, identify diseases, and classify plant species, redefining agriculture practices.

Understand the transformative power of Machine Learning across these sectors. Learn how it enhances software development, revolutionizes transcription, drives retail innovation, empowers marketing strategies, optimizes manufacturing, strengthens cybersecurity, and revolutionizes modern agriculture practices.

ML is helpful in many real-world scenarios. Let's look at some case studies.

CASE STUDIES: HOW MACHINE LEARNING IS
RELEVANT IN TODAY'S WORLD

Let's explore the fascinating world of machine learning
through compelling case studies that showcase its relevance
in today's dynamic landscape. From healthcare to finance
and e-commerce to transportation, these real-world examples illuminate how machine learning shapes industries,
enhances experiences, and drives transformative change.

***Dell's Remarkable Machine Learning Triumph: Boosting
Marketing Impact***

Dell, a global technology leader, partnered with Persado, an
AI and ML-driven marketing technology, to enhance their
email communications and gain data-backed insights. This
collaboration resulted in a remarkable 50% average increase
in Click-Through Rates (CTR), a 46% average rise in
customer responses, a 22% average boost in page visits, and
a striking 77% average surge in add-to-carts (DataFlair,
n.d.).

Inspired by this success, Dell extended machine learning's
influence to their entire marketing spectrum, including
Facebook ads, display banners, direct mail, and radio
content. This journey showcases the transformative power
of machine learning in amplifying marketing strategies,
solidifying Dell's commitment to a data-driven and
impactful marketing future.

Revolutionizing Customer Experiences: Sky's Machine Learning Triumph

Sky UK, a major entertainment player, leveraged machine learning and AI through Adobe Sensei to revolutionize customer engagement. With 22.5 million diverse customers, they utilized hyper-focused segments, delivering tailored interactions and actionable insights that enriched relationships.

Machine learning guided them in personalizing products and services based on individual preferences, bridging customer intelligence with valuable, personalized experiences.

Empowering Trendyol's E-Commerce Dominance

Turkish e-commerce standout Trendyol embraced machine learning and AI by partnering with Liveclicker, a real-time personalization vendor, to enhance customer loyalty and engagement, particularly in sportswear.

Through personalized marketing campaigns, they achieved remarkable results: an impressive 130% surge in conversion rates, 62% growth in response rates, and a 30% increase in click-through rates (DataFlair, n.d.). By connecting with customers personally, Trendyol established a strong bond.

Expanding beyond personalization, their comprehensive strategy, spanning social media, mobile apps, SEO blogs, and celebrity endorsements, continues to redefine their market presence and nurture their customer base.

Revolutionizing Marketing with Harley Davidson: Albert's AI Success

Harley Davidson NYC embraced the AI-powered robot Albert to reshape modern marketing. Albert's fusion of machine learning and AI revolutionized various social media and email channels. Its predictive abilities pinpoint potential converters and adapt creative content dynamically.

Analyzing customer data, Harley Davidson utilized Albert to identify positive behavior patterns, achieving a 40% sales increase and an impressive 2,930% lead boost, with AI-identified "lookalikes" playing a significant role (DataFlair, n.d.).

Elevating User Experience: Yelp's Machine Learning Mastery

Yelp leverages machine learning to enrich its user experience. Its algorithms assist human staff by efficiently managing images through categorization and labeling. These techniques enable attribute identification, like outdoor seating or ambiance, using features such as color and texture.

With a vast image database, Yelp predicts attributes accurately, exceeding 80% (DataFlair, n.d.). It empowers enhanced user experiences and signifies the potential of AI in shaping its future.

In summary, machine learning is an integral part of our daily lives, revolutionizing industries and enhancing user experiences. The impending AI-driven "industrial revolution" envisions machines handling both physical and mental tasks.

In healthcare, it transforms diagnosis, treatment, and prediction, navigating electronic health records for hidden patterns. In finance, it automates processes, improves risk management, and crafts marketing strategies, ensuring fair decision-making. Startups like Signifyd, HyperScience, and FutureAdvisor redefine finance.

Transportation benefits from route optimization and safety enhancements, while machine learning impacts software development, retail, cybersecurity, and agriculture. Real-world case studies highlight its impact, promising further innovations that will shape the future, making daily life more efficient and insightful.

Exploring the multifaceted influence of machine learning across diverse domains, it becomes evident that a comprehensive grasp of the underlying technical terminology and fundamental concepts is essential.

GETTING TECHNICAL: KEY CONCEPTS AND TERMINOLOGIES

The language of Machine Learning may seem daunting, but it's the key to unlocking its immense power. The words we use to talk about Machine Learning might initially sound tricky, but they're like a unique code that helps us understand and use its exceptional abilities.

Think of it like learning a new language. Knowing a language allows us to communicate with people from different places and understand new things. Machine Learning has its language that lets us make computers super smart. This language helps us teach computers to do all sorts of cool things, like recognizing pictures, understanding what we say, and making predictions.

So, even though it may seem challenging at first, learning the language of Machine Learning is like getting the key to unlock its incredible power. Once we understand it, we can use computers in really awesome ways!

UNDERSTANDING THE MACHINE LEARNING PROCESS

Machine learning, a revolutionary concept, enables computers to learn without explicit programming. Imagine machines that learn from data, just like we learn from experiences. To grasp this process, think of it as a lifecycle, a journey that computers embark upon to tackle problems effectively.

Gathering Data: The First Step

Just like we need information to solve a problem, computers require data. This step includes collecting data from various sources like files, databases, and the internet. Think of it as building our project's solid foundation.

Data Preparation: Setting the Stage

Before our computer can learn, we need to organize the data. It means putting it in proper order, like arranging puzzle pieces. We explore the data to understand it better, like learning about the parts before solving the puzzle.

Data Wrangling: Cleaning Up

Data often needs to be more organized. It's like cleaning a room before a party. We remove duplicates, fix errors, and get everything ready for analysis.

Data Analysis: Unveiling Insights

Now comes the magic. We use data analysis techniques to learn from the data. It's like uncovering secrets from a treasure map. We build models that learn from patterns and information in the data.

Training the Model: Teaching the Machine

Our computer model is like a student. We train it using data so that it learns to make predictions. It's like teaching a dog new tricks.

Testing the Model: Checking Its Skills

Like we give tests to students, we test our model's accuracy. We see if it can provide accurate predictions using new information it hasn't seen before.

Deployment: Putting It to Work

Once our model is ready, it's like a superhero ready for action. We deploy it into real-world applications to solve problems. But we're careful–we ensure that it's doing a great job before it starts working.

In simpler words, machine learning is like instructing a computer to learn from experiences. It's like guiding a friend through a journey of understanding, step by step.

Like you learn to ride a bike, machines learn from data to solve problems and make intelligent decisions.

Machine learning doesn't only follow a process, but it has terminologies, too. Let's learn some of them.

KEY TERMINOLOGIES

Machine Learning

In the world of computers, machine learning is all about getting better over time. It's like teaching a computer to improve its skills based on its experiences. This field blends computer science, statistics, and artificial intelligence to create intelligent programs.

Supervised Learning

In supervised learning, a program learns from a set of known data. By studying this data, the program becomes skilled at making accurate decisions when faced with new data. For example, we use a collection of tweets labeled as positive, negative, or neutral to train a sentiment analysis tool. In that case, it can then determine the sentiment of other tweets it encounters.

Unsupervised Learning

Unsupervised learning involves a program that automatically uncovers patterns and relationships within a dataset. Think of it as organizing emails based on similar topics without guidance or training. This technique is called clustering, where the program groups related data together.

Generative Model

A generative model is a tool used in machine learning to create data values when specific details are unknown. This model type is handy for producing likely data combinations by understanding the connections between variables. It's like learning the rules behind a game to predict outcomes or even generate new examples. Examples of generative models include Gaussian Mixture Model, Naive Bayes, and Latent Dirichlet Allocation.

Discriminative Model

Discriminative models focus on understanding the relation-ship between variables, specifically how one variable depends on another. These models calculate the probabili-ties of specific outcomes based on given conditions. For instance, in supervised learning scenarios, they predict one thing based on another, like guessing whether an email is spam or not, depending on its content. Discriminative models encompass techniques such as Neural Networks, Logistic Regression, and Support Vector Machines (SVMs).

Classification

Think of classifying as grouping things into different categories. Imagine you're sorting fruits into baskets based on their type. In the same way, computers create models to sort data into other classes. It helps them predict what category new data belongs to.

Regression

Regression is a means to help understand the connections of different kinds of information. Think about profile pictures on social media–the arrangement of pixels in an image links to a person. It helps machines recognize faces, like when Facebook suggests names for people in your photos.

Regressions are also handy for predicting what could happen using current data. People have been using this technique for a while, like figuring out how someone's brain might recover after a stroke or guessing if customers might leave a telecom company. The cool thing now is that machines can do this predicting stuff faster.

Regression comes in different flavors. One kind, called linear regression, works when dealing with things with a range of values, like prices. Then there's logistic regression, which is like putting things into categories. For instance, it can tell if a store is open (1) or closed (0).

If you want to explore more, there are other types of regression, like random forest regression, decision tree regression, support vector regression, and polynomial regression. You can think of them as distinct tools for understanding and predicting things.

Clustering

Clustering is a unique way that computers learn without being told what to look for. It's like sorting things based on their traits and characteristics.

Clustering helps in various ways. Imagine grouping customers by their shopping habits to offer them better deals or analyzing houses and their locations to decide their value and where to build new areas in a city. It can also organize information in libraries or websites, helping people quickly find what they need.

The most common type of clustering is K-means clustering. It's like saying, "Let's have this many groups," and then finding the center point of each group. All the data points are sorted into groups based on the closest center point. Here are some examples of how to use K-means clustering:

- A hospital figuring out where to put emergency units close to accident-prone areas.
- A scientist studying earthquakes to find places that might be at risk.
- A pizza place deciding where to open new stores based on where people order from the most.

There are other ways to cluster, like density-based, hierarchical, partitioning, and grid-based methods. They are tools for understanding and organizing information.

Association

Think of association as figuring out what things often go together. Computers find patterns in data relationships, like how you might notice people buying ice cream and cones at the same time.

Decision Trees

Decision trees are like making a flowchart for making decisions. They help computers decide based on multiple steps; for example, you might decide whether to play outside depending on the weather.

Support Vector Machines

You can think of Support Vector Machines (SVMs) as drawing lines to divide different things. Imagine drawing lines between different colors of marble to keep them separate.

Neural Networks

Consider neural networks as cousins of deep learning. They create layers of connected brain-like cells called neurons to understand information and give good insights.

Imagine these neurons in layers: one for taking in info, another for doing calculations, and one for giving results. Let's say we're guessing airplane ticket prices. The first layer collects information like where you're flying from and when. Each piece of info gets a "weight" to show its importance. Then, the last layer gives you an estimated ticket price based on all that info.

In a nutshell, neural networks help computers learn and understand stuff just like our brains do.

Deep Learning

Deep learning is like a particular type of machine learning that tries to copy how our brain works. It's all about understanding a lot of organized and messy information and finding patterns. The more information it learns, the better it becomes at making intelligent decisions. Let's see where it's helpful:

- **Talking to Robots:** Think of Siri or Alexa – they can understand what we say and talk back like humans.
- **Smart Ads:** When ads on websites or apps compete, deep learning helps decide which is best, depending on who might be interested and what the weather is like.
- **Giving Recommendations:** Services like Spotify or Netflix suggest what to listen to or watch next based on what we've liked. They use deep learning to make those suggestions super accurate.

So, deep learning is like super-smart technology that learns from lots of data and helps make our gadgets and apps clever.

Reinforcement Learning

Reinforcement learning is like playing a game and improving by trying different moves. Computers learn through trial and error, just like when playing games.

Cross-Validation

Think of cross-validation as a way to ensure that our learning is accurate. It's like trying different methods to solve a puzzle and picking the best one.

Bayesian Approach

In probability, the Bayesian approach is about learning as we gather more information. It's like adjusting your guess about the weather as you get more updates.

Natural Language Processing

You'll often encounter natural language processing when you learn about machine learning. It is a crucial aspect of AI focused on helping computers understand human languages. It's akin to teaching computers how people communicate. It plays a vital role in fields like machine learning and data science. However, it's complex because human speech isn't always direct.

Cultural phrases, unique words, and diverse communication styles add to the challenge. Even sentence structure can alter meaning. Like in human conversations, computers must decipher word meanings and their connections.

Machine Vision

You can think of machine vision as teaching machines to understand pictures. It enables computers to see and analyze images, aiding in tasks like disease detection in medical X-rays and helping self-driving cars identify objects on the road.

Machines can use various methods to "see," like assigning numbers to colors, breaking down images, and recognizing shapes. As machines learn more, they become better at grasping the complete picture. Currently, machine vision is applicable in factories for improved operations and in self-driving cars, drones, and even surgical procedures.

Machine Learning Engineers

With all these remarkable new technologies, who makes them work in actual companies? That's where machine learning engineers come in. They're like tech experts who focus on creating systems that can learn and do things by themselves. These engineers need to know lots of things, like different kinds of code and computer science. So, these engineers are like the wizards who ensure that all these fantastic things we discussed work in the real world.

In summary, Machine Learning is the language that unlocks the remarkable potential of computers, allowing them to learn and make intelligent decisions. It's similar to teaching a friend a new skill, guiding them through a step-by-step journey of understanding.

This process involves gathering, preparing, and analyzing data, training and testing models, and ultimately deploying them. Familiarizing yourself with key terms like supervised learning, deep learning, and clustering is similar to obtaining the key to unlock computers' unique abilities in this exciting field.

Now that you understand the simplified machine learning process and its terminologies, you're ready to learn about algorithms—the heart of machine learning.

FROM THEORY TO PRACTICE: MACHINE LEARNING ALGORITHMS

Just as electricity transformed almost everything 100 years ago, today I actually have a hard time thinking of an industry that I don't think AI will transform in the next several years.

— ANDREW NG

Around 100 years ago, introducing electricity revolutionized daily life, improving lights, machines, and comfort. Now, consider that Artificial Intelligence is akin to advanced computer programs mimicking human thinking. Similar to electricity's impact, AI is reshaping the present.

AI is poised to impact numerous industries and fields in the coming years, just as electricity did. AI's influence spans healthcare, transportation, communication, and education, making processes more intelligent and effective.

Like electricity enhances various aspects of life, AI is an intelligent assistant capable of learning, thinking, and problem-solving.

In this chapter, we'll discuss the building blocks of machine learning that help AI transform industries. Let's start with supervised learning.

SUPERVISED LEARNING

Supervised learning is an artificial intelligence method where a computer program learns by looking at examples. Imagine teaching a computer by showing it pictures with labels or tags. The computer knows to find patterns in these labeled examples. So, when it sees new pictures without labels, it can guess the correct label based on what it has learned.

This learning type is like solving puzzles. You have pieces with labels and learn how they fit together. In AI, this helps the computer understand and solve specific questions. It's good at tasks like sorting things into categories, deciding if an email is spam, or predicting future things like how many products a store might sell on a specific day.

Companies use supervised learning to catch unusual things, like spotting fraud in transactions. It's like teaching the computer to see and understand things as we do.

How Supervised Learning Works

Supervised learning is like teaching a computer how to solve problems using examples. Imagine you're showing it pictures and telling it what's in those pictures. The computer learns from these examples and determines how things are connected. Once it remembers well, it can guess what's in new photos without labels.

Here's how it works:

1. **Getting Ready:** The computer needs labeled data, like pictures with descriptions. It learns from these examples.
2. **Training Phase:** The computer looks at the labeled examples and learns how things are connected. It tries to find relationships and patterns between the input (the pictures) and the output (the labels).
3. **Testing Phase:** Now, the computer undergoes testing. It's given new pictures with hidden labels. The computer's job is to guess the labels based on what it learned.
4. **Accuracy Check:** The next phase involves checking the computer's guesses. If it guesses right most of the time, it's accurate.

Imagine teaching a friend how to recognize cats and dogs. You show them many pictures, and they learn to tell them apart. Then you give them new photos to test how well they learned.

However, like when you learn something new, you must practice and ensure that you don't make mistakes. Computers do the same thing. They practice with different sets of data and improve their accuracy over time.

It's like training a superhero to know which villains are good or bad just by looking at them. The superhero improves with practice and can tell the villains apart even if they've never seen them.

Types of Supervised Learning Algorithms

Supervised learning algorithms have two kinds: regression and classification.

Classification Algorithms

Imagine sorting things into different groups based on how they look. That's what classification algorithms do. They use the labeled examples they classified to sort things into different categories. For instance, they can decide if a picture is of a dog or a cat or if an email is spam. Examples of classification techniques include:

- **Decision Tree:** It's like a tree that separates things into smaller and smaller groups, like sorting animals based on their features.

- **Logistic Regression:** It determines if something belongs to one of two groups, like deciding whether a review is positive or negative.
- **Random Forest:** This is like a collection of decision trees working together, like asking many friends to help determine whether a movie is good.
- **Support Vector Machine:** It draws a line to separate things into different groups, for example, dividing students into those who like math and those who prefer art.

Regression Models

These are like predicting numbers based on patterns. For instance, guessing a house's price based on its location. Examples of regression models include:

- **Linear Regression:** It's like drawing a straight line through data points to predict what comes next.
- **Nonlinear Regression:** This model is helpful when data points don't follow a straight line, like when something goes up and down again. The stock market is a prime example that uses this model.
- **Regression Tree:** Think of it as a tree that tells you how much something could cost based on its features.

When choosing a supervised learning method, consider the algorithm's balance between adaptability and becoming too adaptable. Also, think about the complexity of the model needed and assess data qualities like diversity, precision, repetitiveness, and straightness.

Strive for a balance between adaptability and consistency, evaluate the algorithm's suitability for your problem's complexity and data characteristics, and remember that different data types require a well-matched algorithm.

Now that you understand the supervised learning types, your next goal is to understand its advantages and disadvantages.

Pros and Cons of Supervised Learning

In navigating the world of machine learning, it's critical to know the strengths and limitations of different approaches. Supervised learning, a fundamental technique, offers both advantages and disadvantages.

Let's explore the pros and cons of this approach to better appreciate its potential and challenges in artificial intelligence.

✛ Advantages:

- Supervised learning is like learning from past experiences. It helps us gather information and make predictions based on our knowledge. It makes it easier to improve how well something works.

- It's excellent at improving things by using what it learned before.
- Supervised learning is super helpful in solving many real-life problems that involve computers.
- It helps sort things into groups or predict numbers– like telling if an email is good or bad or guessing how much something costs.
- Based on our knowledge, it helps us guess what could happen with new things.
- We can decide how many groups we want to use in the training data.

— **Disadvantages:**

- Dealing with Big Data can take time and effort.
- Learning in supervised ways takes a lot of time on computers.
- It can't solve all the complicated problems in machine learning.
- It takes time for computers to excel in performance.
- It can't handle things without labels–it needs to know the names of things.
- Teaching the computer takes time and effort.

Use Case of Supervised Learning

Imagine using computers to sort news articles into business, technology, or sports categories. It helps us find exciting news. For this task, supervised learning can be advantageous. It can teach the computer to read many news articles and categorize them.

However, sometimes the categories don't cover everything. Some news articles talk about different things at once. So, instead of using fixed types, we can use unsupervised learning. It helps the computer find similar news articles and group them without needing selected categories. It's like the computer is finding patterns in the news.

UNSUPERVISED LEARNING

Think of unsupervised learning like a computer exploring on its own. Just like when you learn new things without someone telling you what's right or wrong, unsupervised learning lets the computer find patterns in data without being told what to look for.

Unsupervised learning helps computers find hidden patterns in data without being guided. It's like a puzzle where the computer figures out how things fit together. It enables grouping similar items and showing data more straightforwardly.

For example, if a computer is given many pictures of cats and dogs but doesn't know what they are, unsupervised learning helps it sort them into groups based on their appearance. It's like the computer is learning independently, just like how you figure out things when you explore.

Importance of Unsupervised Learning

Unsupervised machine learning searches for hidden patterns in data, though its results often aren't as accurate as supervised learning. This is because supervised learning uses known outcomes to improve accuracy. Unsupervised learning is valuable when you don't know the results, like finding a target market for a new product. But for understanding your existing customers, supervised learning is better.

Unsupervised learning has applications like:

- **Clustering:** It groups similar data. However, it can sometimes group things too similarly.
- **Anomaly Detection:** It finds unusual data points helpful in catching fraud or errors.
- **Association Mining:** It identifies things that go together, which is helpful for retailers to plan marketing.
- **Latent Variable Models:** These help with reducing data complexity.

The patterns from unsupervised learning can also help in other types of knowledge, like using cluster groups as extra info for supervised learning or anomaly scores for detecting fraud.

Kinds of Unsupervised Learning Algorithms

Independent learning has two main types:

- **Clustering:** Imagine putting similar things together. Clustering groups things that are alike. It finds everyday things and sorts them into groups. It's like organizing toys into groups based on their attributes.
- **Association:** This is about finding things that often go together. It's like knowing that people who buy bread, buy butter or jam, too. It helps in making better marketing plans. For example, if you see people buying a specific item, you can suggest another thing that usually goes with it.

In simple words, unsupervised learning helps computers find patterns in data and figure out how things are related. The device sorts things based on what they have in common.

Clustering

Clustering is like sorting things into groups based on their resemblances or disparities. There are a few types of clustering, each with its way of organizing data.

Exclusive and Overlapping Clustering

Exclusive clustering means that items are only in one group. It's like putting toys in separate boxes. K-means clustering is an example where data points come in groups based on their distance from a center point. It's helpful in organizing things like information and images.

Hierarchical Clustering

Hierarchical clustering puts things together step-by-step. It can start with separate groups and combine them based on similarities. It can be like building a family tree, where you start with people and keep connecting them based on who's related to each other.

Probabilistic Clustering

It is like finding the chance of something belonging to a specific group. Gaussian Mixture Model (GMM) is a standard method. It figures out which group a thing might belong to based on the chances that it's part of a specific distribution, like finding out if a shape is most like a circle, square, or triangle.

These methods help computers understand and group data differently, making it easier to see patterns and relationships. It's like organizing things in your room based on how they look or work together.

Association

Association rules are like discovering patterns between things in a dataset. Think of it as finding out that when people buy bread, they often purchase butter, too. It helps companies recommend something you might like, just like Amazon suggests items based on your purchase.

Imagine that you're listening to music on Spotify. If you start with a song by one band, the app might recommend a piece from a similar band. The app knows what people like you usually listen to using algorithms like Apriori.

Apriori Algorithms

These algorithms help companies understand what things people usually buy or do together. They are helpful in places like online shops and music apps. They make recommendations based on what other people with similar tastes have done. It's like suggesting that you might like a new toy based on the toys you already have. These algorithms use a unique way of counting things to figure out the patterns.

Pros and Cons of Unsupervised Learning

Diving into machine learning, understanding the merits and drawbacks of different approaches is crucial. Unsupervised learning, a powerful technique, presents both advantages and limitations. Exploring the method's pros and cons sheds light on its potential and challenges in the exciting world of artificial intelligence.

✚ Advantages

- Unsupervised learning tackles complex tasks, since it deals with data without labels, making it suitable for challenging problems.
- It's preferred because finding unlabeled data is more accessible than finding labeled data.

━ Disadvantages

- Unlike supervised learning, unsupervised learning is more complicated, as it needs precise output data to learn from.
- Results might not be as accurate because the algorithms work with unlabeled data and can't predict the exact output.

Use Cases of Unsupervised Learning

Machine learning methodologies have become widely used for improving user experiences and testing system quality. Unsupervised learning is a way to explore data, helping businesses find patterns in large amounts of data faster than doing it manually. Here are some everyday ways of using unsupervised learning:

- **News Sorting:** Google News uses unsupervised learning to combine news articles about the same topic, like grouping stories about a presidential election.
- **Seeing With Computers:** Unsupervised learning helps computers recognize things in pictures, like telling if a photo has a cat or a dog.
- **Medical Images:** It helps doctors quickly see essential things in medical images like X-rays, making it easier to diagnose patients.
- **Finding Odd Things:** Unsupervised learning can find strange things in a lot of data, like spotting a broken machine or a security problem.
- **Knowing Customers:** It helps businesses understand their customers' habits, like determining who buys certain products and why.
- **Smart Recommendations:** How do online shops suggest products you like? Unsupervised learning looks at what you and others bought before and offers similar things.

Unsupervised learning makes computers better understand things and helps businesses give you what you want.

REINFORCED LEARNING

Reinforced Learning (RL) is a technique for making intelligent choices, like mastering a game strategy. Just as children learn through trial and error, RL involves a computer exploring various actions to achieve optimal outcomes.

The computer, operating independently, identifies the best action sequence, similar to finding the right path for maximum rewards. It considers both immediate and delayed rewards, enabling success in unfamiliar scenarios. RL is exciting, as it empowers computers to self-learn and excel in problem-solving.

How Reinforced Learning Works

In Reinforced Learning, an agent is like a learner trying to achieve a goal in an unknown world. It believes that it can reach all destinations by getting the most rewards. The agent communicates with the environment, using actions to get the most premiums. Think of it like someone playing a game to win.

RL has the following vital elements:

- **The Agent:** That's the one trying to learn and get rewards.
- **The Environment:** That's where the agent plays and learns.

- **The Policy:** This is like the agent's plan of action. It decides what steps to take.
- **The Reward Signal:** This is like a score. The agent gets rewards for reasonable efforts.

The value function is like a measure of how good a situation is. It looks at the immediate reward and the rewards that come later. The agent aims to find the best actions to get the most premiums.

Types of Reinforced Learning Algorithms

There are three main ways to use reinforced learning in machine learning:

Value-Based Approach

- This approach is like figuring out the best values for different situations.
- The agent wants to know how much reward it can get in the long run at other places.
- It's like studying a board game and deciding which moves are best for winning.

Policy-Based Approach

- Here, the focus is on finding the best strategies for getting many future rewards.
- The agent tries to follow a plan (policy) that helps it get the most benefits.
- It can always do the same thing at a specific place or choose actions with certain chances.

Model-Based Approach

- In this approach, the agent makes a pretend model of the environment and learns from that.
- It's like making a fake world to practice in and get better.
- There's no fixed solution for this because the agent applies different knowledge for each situation.

So, using these approaches, the agent learns to make the best decisions and get the most rewards in different situations.

Pros and Cons of Reinforced Learning

Reinforcement learning offers exciting possibilities in training AI to achieve goals autonomously, but it has advantages and challenges. Let's explore the benefits and drawbacks of reinforcement learning, diving into how it empowers machines to learn by trial and error in complex environments.

+ Advantages

Reinforced learning (RL) is like a superhero algorithm that can handle challenging problems that other machine learning methods struggle with. It's almost like an intelligent friend that can think for himself and figure out how to achieve big goals over time. Some fantastic things about RL include:

- **Seeing the Big Picture:** RL tackles the whole thing, unlike other machine learning methods focusing on small parts of a problem. It aims to get the best results, even if it means giving up some immediate rewards.
- **Learning by Doing:** RL agents don't need someone to instruct them. They learn through interaction and exploration of their environment, like how you learn by trying things out.
- **Handling Changes:** RL is a quick learner. It can adjust to changes in its surroundings and keep getting better.

⸺ Disadvantages

While Reinforced Learning is fantastic, it also faces some tough challenges:

1. **Need for Experience:** RL agents need much experience to become good at something. Sometimes, the environment they're in can slow down their learning process.
2. **Delayed Rewards:** RL agents care about the big picture, making it hard to understand which actions led to which results, especially if the results take a while to show up.
3. **Hard to Explain:** Sometimes, it's not easy to understand why an RL agent makes certain decisions. This lack of clarity can make trusting and working with them tricky.

So, while RL has its superhero strengths, it also faces real-world challenges that require solutions.

Use Cases of Reinforced Learning

Reinforced learning (RL) is the magical ingredient that helps computers play tricky games like chess, Go, and shogi (Japanese chess). Imagine DeepMind using RL to create AlphaGo, a computer application that crushed a human Go champion! From there, they made AlphaZero, a super-intelligent AI that learned chess so well that it beat the famous chess engine Stockfish in four hours.

AlphaZero comprises an innovative neural network and a clever Monte Carlo Tree Search algorithm. It differs from Deep Blue, the 1997 supercomputer that beat a human chess champion. Deep Blue used lots of computing power to examine chess moves quickly. But AlphaZero uses its neural network and intelligent algorithms to learn and play well.

People also use deep RL to help crewless spacecraft explore new places, like Mars or the moon. There's a tremendous project called MarsExplorer, where scientists train AI to navigate tricky terrain. They're using four different AI algorithms, and one called PPO is doing well. It is a big step in helping robots explore unknown places safely.

Reinforced Learning is also helping self-driving cars learn how to drive, predict stock prices in the finance world, and even diagnose rare diseases in healthcare. It's teaching computers to do amazing things that humans are still figuring out.

In summary, Artificial Intelligence (AI) is a transformative force with wide-reaching impacts on various industries, including healthcare, transportation, and communication.

Among AI's core components, supervised learning stands out as a fundamental element of machine learning, allowing computers to learn from patterns and provide specific answers. While it excels in tasks like spam detection and sales prediction, it presents challenges in handling large datasets and time constraints.

Unsupervised learning involves computers autonomously discovering patterns and organizing data, useful for finding hidden relationships but facing accuracy and data complexity issues.

Reinforced Learning (RL) takes AI a step further by teaching computers to make intelligent decisions based on rewards. AI, similar to the impact of electricity, is shaping the world, and supervised and reinforcement learning are pivotal tools in this transformative journey, enabling innovation and problem-solving.

Now that we have a grasp of the essential foundations of machine learning through algorithms, let's shift our focus to something equally crucial—the energy that drives these algorithms forward.

DATA: THE FUEL OF MACHINE LEARNING

O ver 2.5 quintillion data bytes exist daily, fueling machine learning (Price, n.d.). This data influx enables machines to learn and improve their performance, leading to better insights and outcomes across various fields.

This chapter will explore data's vital role in data processing techniques and machine learning. You'll learn its significance in ML and how to prepare for successful machine learning implementation.

THE IMPORTANCE OF DATA

Data holds a vital role in Machine Learning. It involves the collection of measurements or observations that teach a machine-learning model. The quantity and quality of data used for testing and training significantly impact a model's performance.

Data can take diverse forms like numbers, categories, or time sequences and can come from different places like databases or spreadsheets. Machine learning relies on data to recognize patterns between input and output, helping with predictions or classifications.

Types of Data in Machine Learning

When working with machine learning, we use different kinds of data to help algorithms make predictions. Let's discuss the main data types we use and make them simpler to understand.

- **Categorical Data:** This type of data groups things into categories. For example, think about car colors, like green, blue, or silver. Since these aren't numbers but different categories, we call it categorical data. We turn it into numbers for the computer to understand, using "one hot encoding."
- **Numerical Data:** This is all about numbers. We have features (like "attack" and "defense") and associated numerical values. These could be decimals, but they're still numbers. Sometimes, a dataset might have both numbers and categories.
- **Time Series Data:** We use time-related info to improve machine learning. We take certain values

over specific periods and connect them to our data. It's like having a timeline. This time-based info can help our predictions be more accurate.

- **Text Data:** Consider all the text in posts and articles. We use machine learning on them, too. We turn this text into numbers using special tricks so the computer can understand. Imagine turning a sentence into numbers and letting the computer find patterns.

Different types of data help machines understand and predict things. It's like teaching the machine to see patterns and make intelligent choices.

Advantages and Disadvantages of Using Data in Machine Learning

Using data in machine learning offers numerous advantages, such as enhanced accuracy, automation of tasks, personalized experiences, and cost savings. However, there are drawbacks, including data quality issues, privacy concerns, potential bias, and challenges in interpreting complex models.

Let's explore these benefits and drawbacks to better understand data's role in machine learning.

+ Pros:

- **Better Accuracy:** When machines have lots of data, they can learn more about how things are connected. This connection helps them make better predictions and decisions.
- **Automation:** Machine learning can do tasks automatically and well. It's like having a competent assistant who doesn't get tired of repetitive work.
- **Personal Touch:** Machines use data to give you personalized experiences. Think of it like getting a movie recommendation that you'll probably love.
- **Saving Money:** Machine learning can help businesses save money by doing work that humans used to do. It makes things faster and cheaper.

— Cons:

- **Bias Issues:** Sometimes, the training data is one-sided, making the machine's decisions unfair or wrong.
- **Privacy Concerns:** Gathering and storing data can be a privacy problem. Mishandling can result in misused or stolen data.
- **Data Quality Matters:** If the data used isn't good, the machine's predictions won't be, either. Poor-quality data means bad results.
- **Hard to Understand:** Some machines make decisions that are hard to understand. It's like

having an intelligent friend who doesn't always explain why they think a certain way.

Remember, using data in machine learning can be super helpful, but we must be careful about how we use it to ensure fairness, privacy, and accuracy.

How Much Data Does Machine Learning Need?

The amount of data is crucial to remember when dealing with machine learning. Finding the right balance is vital: We need enough data so the machine doesn't struggle, but not too much to overwhelm it—just like humans need the right amount of food.

Sometimes, we're short on data. In such cases, we can gather more data through surveys or questionnaires. If that's impossible, there are other techniques, like data augmentation, where we create more data for the machine to learn from.

Sometimes, we have excess data. In these situations, it's essential to keep valuable information. One technique is to use all the information in separate rounds of training. It lets the machine learn from different parts of the data while keeping a bit of it each time. For example, the first round of training used ¾ of the data. The second round will also use ¾ of the data, but this time, it will include the other ¼ unused by the previous one.

When we train a machine, it's like students preparing for exams. We leave some data for testing, just as we test students. The data used for testing—testing data—stays hidden from the machine until testing. It helps us see how well the device has learned.

How Machines Learn From Data

When we train a machine, we give it lots of data to study. It looks at each piece of data, learns patterns from it, and remembers those patterns. Later, when we want the machine to make predictions, it uses what it learned from the data.

Imagine predicting the weather. The machine takes past data and figures out how temperature links to outcomes. For instance, when we want to know the weather tomorrow, we give the device some details, like temperature. It then uses what it learned earlier to provide us with a prediction.

Machines learn from data and use that learning to guess what might happen next. If the guess is correct, the device has understood well. If it's wrong, there's room to get better. Just like people, machines make mistakes, too. The object is to make fewer mistakes over time and to be as accurate as possible.

Remember, getting the right amount of data is like giving the machine the right amount of fuel—it helps it perform at its best. However, before using data, it has to undergo preprocessing and extraction, which we'll discuss next.

DATA PREPROCESSING AND FEATURE EXTRACTION

Data preprocessing and feature extraction are vital to preparing data for machine learning. Data preprocessing involves organizing, transforming, and cleaning raw data to ensure its suitability and quality for analysis. Feature extraction focuses on selecting and creating meaningful features from the data. It boosts the performance of machine learning models. We'll discuss each model in this section.

Data preprocessing involves steps to prepare data for machines to understand easily. For a model to predict accurately, it must understand the data's features well. Real-world data can have problems, like missing parts or errors due to different sources. If we don't clean this data, the results can be wrong.

Removing duplicate or missing values is crucial. Strange data can also mess up learning. Good decisions come from good data. Preprocessing makes data suitable. Without it, it's like putting trash in and expecting good results.

Data Preprocessing Steps

Let's explore the crucial steps of data preprocessing in more detail.

Data Cleaning

To clean data means to prepare it for machines. It includes filling in missing parts, eliminating noise, fixing mistakes, and removing unusual data points.

- **Missing Values:** Sometimes, data is incomplete. We can either ignore it or guess the missing parts using unique methods.
- **Noisy Data:** Errors in data can include static on a call. We can fix this by removing the noise.
- **Outliers:** Some data points are too strange. We might remove them to produce the correct output.

Data Integration

This step is about combining data from different places into one extensive collection. It's like gathering data from other hospitals for a medical study.

Data Transformation

After cleaning and putting data together, we might need to change how it looks or behaves to make it worthwhile. Transforming data is possible through these methods:

- **Generalization:** Turning specific categories into broader categories, like city to country.
- **Normalization:** Scaling numbers to a particular range for comparison.
- **Attribute Selection:** Creating new data from existing data to help machines understand better.
- **Aggregation:** Summarizing data more efficiently.

Data Reduction

Sometimes, data is too big. Reducing it without losing important information is the goal. This can be done by:

- **Data Cube Aggregation:** Summarizing data.
- **Dimensionality Reduction:** Making data more straightforward by using only essential parts.
- **Data Compression**: Shrinking data using unique methods.
- **Discretization:** Dividing continuous data into smaller groups.
- **Numerosity Reduction:** Using models or equations instead of tons of data.
- **Attribute Subset Selection:** Choosing only the essential data.

Data Quality Assessment

Assessing data quality is about checking it to ensure that it's good enough to use.

Data Quality Assessment involves several key elements:

- Ensuring completeness by eliminating missing attribute values.
- Upholding accuracy and reliability in the information provided.
- Ensuring consistency across all data features.
- Maintaining data validity to ensure its relevance and correctness.
- Eliminating any redundancy within the data.

These components collectively ensure the integrity and reliability of the data, which is crucial for informed decision-making and effective data utilization:

- **Data Profiling:** Studying data for issues.
- **Data Cleaning:** Fixing issues.
- **Data Monitoring:** Keeping data clean and checking if it meets the business' needs.

Remember, data preprocessing is like getting your ingredients ready before cooking. It helps machines make tasty predictions!

Feature Extraction

Feature extraction is like tidying up a big mess. It can be challenging for computers to handle when we have lots of data with many details. So, we group some of these details to make it easier. This grouping makes the data simpler but still keeps the essential parts.

Imagine having a lot of toys scattered around. If we put similar toys in a box, it's easier to manage. Feature extraction does the same with data. It helps computers process things faster and learn better by focusing on important stuff.

Uses of Feature Extraction in Machine Learning

Feature extraction is like cleaning up clutter for better machine learning. Here's how it helps:

- **Removing Unnecessary Data:** Think of it as cleaning up a messy room. Feature extraction throws out stuff that doesn't matter, letting the machine focus on essential things.
- **Getting Accurate Results:** Like studying what you need for a test, feature extraction ensures that the machine learns only what's crucial, making its predictions more accurate.
- **Learning Faster:** Just like skipping extra details in a story, using only the critical data helps the machine learn quickly and make better guesses.

- **Saving Energy:** It's like using a flashlight only where you need it. By removing extra data, the device uses less energy and works faster, making it more useful.

Feature Extraction Methods

Scientists use various ways to make raw data useful. Let's explore three standard methods:

- **Image Processing:** This uses algorithms to find interesting things in pictures. It helps machines understand edges, shapes, and movements in images. This info can then help it study or analyze images.
- **Bag of Words:** This is like counting how often words appear in texts, like web pages or social media. It helps computers understand and even create human language.
- **Autoencoders:** These are like magic data cleaners. They squash data, clean it up, and then put it back together. It makes data simpler, helping the computer focus on essential bits.

Each method has its particular use in making data more understandable for computers.

Challenges in Using Feature Extraction in Machine Learning

While machine learning is powerful, some obstacles prevent its smooth implementation:

- **Messy Data Handling:** Preparing data is crucial, but using low-quality data gives terrible results. A poorly-designed or too-complex process of preparing data can affect the outcome.
- **Need for More Resources:** Machine learning needs a lot of computer power. Some organizations need more resources to run these programs alongside their regular tasks.
- **Scattered Data:** For machine learning to work well, lots of data should be in one place, but many organizations have their data spread out in different places, making it hard to see the whole picture.
- **Not Using Automation:** Automation in machine learning can save time. It's like having a helpful assistant. But some don't use it fully, missing the chance to focus on more vital activities.

These challenges can slow down the use of machine learning, but addressing them can make things smoother.

DATA QUALITY ISSUES

When working with machine learning, there are three common data quality challenges to overcome:

- **Incomplete and Inconsistent Data:** Sometimes, data is missing or messy because forms aren't well-controlled. Machine learning relies on patterns, so missing or inconsistent information confuses it. For example, if addresses lack zip codes or are inconsistent, machine learning might struggle to understand where something is.
- **Duplicate Data:** Having the same data repeatedly messes with machine learning's results. It happens with the combination of data from various sources. If records are unmarked as unique, the same thing might be seen as distinct, making machine learning's predictions unreliable.
- **Data Integration and Storage:** Organizations use many tools to accumulate data. However, different formats and places make this tough. For example, if you want to predict customer behavior, you need data from various tools, and putting it all together is a challenge.

Fixing these issues is vital to make machine learning work well. It's like ensuring that all puzzle pieces fit perfectly.

ENSURING DATA QUALITY

In the world of ever-evolving technology, we see more and more demand for new and improved machine learning models. These models need accurate and fast training, and that's where high-quality data comes in. At the beginning of the AI journey, it's crucial to have top-notch data during the data-sourcing stage. If the data isn't good, the model can go wrong or might not work.

To make sure data is high quality:

- It has to be accurate and meet quality standards.
- It should have all the correct info for the machine learning model.
- Data sets must be complete without missing pieces.

To ensure this, we need to monitor the data as we get it and train our models. By checking at different stages, we can guarantee that the data is labeled right and has everything we need. If we need better data, we can quickly get it and keep our project on track.

Imagine that technology is like a hungry creature that needs feeding with data. Not all foods are the same, and not all data is equal. Companies use data to make intelligent decisions, like people choosing healthy foods. However, getting good data takes work.

Data science, which has been around since the 1980s, helps us make sense of data. Think of it as understanding the ingredients in cooking before using them. If you search online, you'll find advice on getting better data. It includes using old concepts like accuracy and new ones like computer programs to clean data.

Here are five steps you can follow to ensure high-quality data.

1. **Define What You Need:** Your data needs to be helpful, like having good ingredients for a recipe. It means you have to decide what "useful data" is. Think about how accurate it is, how complete it is, and if it contains the correct information.
2. **Study Your Data:** Analyze your data to know how it's connected and what rules it follows.
3. **Make Standards:** Just like having rules for cooking, you need rules for data. These rules help everyone understand the data easily. Some rules are standard, like how to write dates. Others are specific to your company.
4. **Connect the Dots:** Consider combining all the ingredients to make a dish. Your data has different parts that are connected. Show these connections so people can understand and use the data better.
5. **Monitor the Data:** Just like checking if your food is cooked right, you must keep checking your data.

Make sure it's still good and valuable. Sometimes data can become old or wrong, like food going bad.

Following these steps ensures that your data is healthy and valuable, just like a good meal.

In summary, data is the lifeblood of Machine Learning, profoundly influencing the performance of models. It takes various forms, from numerical and categorical data to time sequences and text, sourced from diverse origins.

Machine learning relies on data to identify patterns and make precise predictions. While data usage offers benefits like improved accuracy and automation, challenges such as bias, privacy concerns, and data quality issues exist.

Striking the right data balance is crucial. Training models with data allows them to learn and minimize errors, while data preprocessing and feature extraction enhance machine learning efficiency. High-quality data is essential, requiring organizations to define needs, standardize, and monitor data continuously.

High-quality data is an unequivocal prerequisite for the optimal functioning of machine learning. Equipped with a firm grasp of the significance and groundwork involved in data handling, you are now prepared to start a captivating venture—constructing your inaugural machine learning model.

HANDS-ON MACHINE LEARNING: BUILDING YOUR FIRST MODEL

Are you ready to get your hands dirty and build your first Machine Learning model? Let's start the journey of creating your inaugural ML model. Through hands-on experience, you'll unravel the magic of algorithms, data, and patterns. Embrace this opportunity to gain invaluable skills and shape your understanding of AI.

Let's start by learning how to choose the right tools and libraries.

CHOOSING THE RIGHT TOOLS AND LIBRARIES

Selecting the right tools and libraries for machine learning is crucial. They're like skilled helpers that make complex tasks more manageable. Moreover, they ensure efficiency and accuracy in creating Machine Learning models. Just as a craftsman chooses the best tools, your choices impact your success.

Becoming proficient in these tools allows you to manipulate data, train your models, uncover novel techniques, and design algorithms. Various tools, software, and platforms are dedicated to machine learning, and fresh ones are emerging regularly.

Amidst this plethora of options, selecting the optimal tool for your specific model presents a challenge. Picking the appropriate tool can significantly boost the speed and efficiency of your model's development. This section will explore several well-known and frequently utilized machine learning tools and their features.

Machine learning tools are like powerful helpers, making training and creating innovative computer programs much more straightforward. These tools are essential for building apps for making independent predictions. Consider them the vital instruments in your toolbox for creating smart apps.

Tools Helpful in Creating Your Apps

TensorFlow

TensorFlow is a unique library that helps computers learn and understand things from data—many people excited about making machines smart use it. You can think of it as a toolkit with everything you need to teach your computer to do clever things. It's perfect for building apps that understand pictures, sounds, and numbers.

PyTorch

PyTorch is another innovative toolkit. Just like TensorFlow, it helps you teach your computer to recognize patterns and learn from data. It's like a remarkable book that enables you to understand how to make your computer see and understand the world around it. It's convenient for building apps that understand pictures and words.

Google Cloud ML Engine

Sometimes, you need a powerful computer to teach your app new things. That's where Google Cloud ML Engine comes in. It's a super-smart computer that helps your app learn and remember a lot of information. This tool ensures that your app becomes super smart and doesn't tire even when learning from a lot of data.

Amazon Machine Learning (AML)

Amazon also has a tool for building smart apps. It's like a guide that helps you teach your computer to understand and predict things. This tool is great for making apps that can look at different information and guess what might happen next.

Accord.Net

Accord.Net is a toolkit that helps you build computer programs to listen to sounds, look at pictures, and do math.

It's like a special box of tools that makes it easy to create apps that tell you what they see and hear.

Apache Mahout

Apache Mahout is like a big box of math tricks that helps you create computer programs that can learn from data. It's perfect for building apps to find patterns and make predictions based on the information.

Shogun

Shogun is a helpful software library that lets you build apps from examples. It's like a teacher showing your app many examples so it can figure out things independently. This tool is good for creating apps that can make smart decisions and understand patterns.

Oryx2

Oryx2 is like a puzzle solver for making apps that can learn and predict things in real time. It's great for building apps that quickly understand and use new information to make quick decisions.

Apache Spark MLlib

Apache Spark MLlib is like a wizard's book of spells for creating apps that learn and make predictions. It's good at handling and turning lots of information into intelligent insights. This tool is perfect for making apps that can do smart things with a lot of data.

Google ML Kit for Mobile

Google's ML kit is like a superhero toolkit for mobile app developers. It gives them special powers to make apps that recognize faces, read text, and even understand languages. It's excellent for creating apps that can do extraordinary things on your phone, even when you're off the internet.

Python

Python, brought to life by Guido Van Rossum in 1991, is a versatile and friendly programming language. It's like a tool that helps people communicate with computers by giving them clear instructions. Python is unique because it focuses on making code easy to read and understand, even if you're just starting. Learning Python doesn't take as long as other computer languages, making it great for beginners.

Being open source means that Python has grown a lot over time by adding new tools, like extra features in a toolbox. It makes Python useful for crunching numbers, studying statistics, building websites, and working with text. And because Python has been around for quite a while, a large number of people use it and help each other. If you ever get stuck or need help, you can search online or ask questions on websites where experts gather to help people.

So, these machine learning tools are like friends that help you teach computers to do smart things. They provide you with unique abilities to make your apps intelligent and capable of understanding the world around them.

How to Choose the Right ML Framework

You can decide whether to make a unique machine learning framework or select one that already exists to suit your needs. If you're thinking about picking the proper machine-learning framework for your project, consider the following:

Understand Your Needs

When you begin your search for a machine learning framework, consider these three questions:

- Will you use the ML framework for traditional machine or deep learning methods?
- Which programming language do you want to use to create AI models?
- What hardware, software, and cloud services will you use to handle larger tasks?

Python and R are common languages in machine learning, but others like C, Java, and Scala exist. Although statisticians created R, it's becoming less popular due to its complexity. Python, a more modern language, offers simplicity and ease of use.

Optimizing Parameters

Machine learning algorithms use various techniques to understand training data and apply that understanding to new situations.

These algorithms have parameters, like settings, that control how the algorithm works. They tweak how they consider variables, determine the influence of unusual data points, and make other adjustments. When choosing a machine learning framework, consider whether you want these adjustments to happen automatically or if you prefer manual control.

Managing Scaling for Training and Deployment

During the training phase of creating AI algorithms, scalability involves quickly handling and analyzing large amounts of data. Distributed algorithms, processing methods, and hardware like graphics processing units (GPUs) can improve scalability.

In the deployment phase, scalability relates to how many users or applications can use the model at the same time.

Since training and deployment have different needs, organizations usually develop models in one environment (such as using Python-based frameworks in the cloud) and then use them in another environment with strict performance and availability demands, like an on-premises data center.

When choosing a framework, consider whether it can handle both types of scalability and if it supports the environments that you plan to use for development and production.

Considering these factors can allow you to make a smart choice when selecting a machine-learning framework for your project. Now that you know the tools that you can use and how to pick the proper framework, your next goal is to learn how to select an algorithm.

CHOOSING AN ALGORITHM

In Chapter 4, you learned about the various algorithms you can use for Machine Learning. This section will discuss picking the one that is best suited to your needs.

Step 1: Know Your Goal for the ML Project

Each machine-learning algorithm can solve a specific problem. So, start by considering your current project. What outcome do you want? Consider supervised forecasting algorithms if you need to predict based on past data. If you're dealing with image recognition for not-so-great images, a mix of dimensionality reduction and classification could help. Want to teach your model a new game? Try a reinforcement algorithm.

Step 2: Scrutinize Your Data by Annotation, Procedure, and Size

Once you know your desired output, think about your input data. What's your data like? Is it raw and messy, needing some cleaning up? Is it unorganized and needs structuring? Do you have a well-labeled dataset? Have you gathered sufficient data? Consider preparing your data before training, especially if it's not in great shape. Unsupervised algorithms could work if you're short on data, but they have limits.

Step 3: Evaluate the Training Time and Speed

Think about the speed you need from your algorithm. Do you need quick results, even if they're less accurate? Remember, more and better data usually leads to better training. Can you dedicate the necessary time for thorough training?

Step 4: Determine Your Data Linearity

Consider the nature of your problem. Linear algorithms, like support vectors or linear regression machines, are simpler and quicker to train. However, they work well only with linear data. If your data is complex, with many different aspects and connections, linear methods might be insufficient.

Step 5: Determine the Number of Parameters and Features

Lastly, think about how complex and accurate you want your AI model to be. Remember that more extended training often means a more precise model when used. If you have the time, you can give your algorithm more features and parameters to learn from, leading to better accuracy.

Following these steps, you can select the correct machine-learning algorithm for your project's success.

IMPLEMENTING A SIMPLE ML MODEL

Machine learning models are compelling tools for solving complex problems and handling vital tasks. With the growing amount of data worldwide, different types of organizations are eager to use machine learning models. These models find applications in various sectors, from monitoring bank transfers for fraud to enhancing diagnostic tools in healthcare.

Building a machine learning model might seem complicated, but experts in data science do it often. However, you should understand the process as you adopt this technology. This guide explores the six manageable steps in developing a machine-learning model.

1. Contextualize Machine Learning in Your Organization

Understand why your organization needs a machine learning model. Having clear goals is essential so that everyone knows what the model will achieve. Deciding on project owners, problem definition, and data sources are vital tasks at this stage.

2. Perform Data Analysis and Pick the Most Appropriate Algorithm

Look at your data and determine what algorithm would work best. Different types of tasks and data require different approaches. Data exploration helps scientists understand the data better and choose the correct algorithm.

3. Prepare and Clean the Dataset

High-quality training data is essential for a good model. Data must undergo cleaning, standardization, and checking for missing or unusual values. It is the foundation for practical model training.

4. Split the Prepared Dataset and Perform Cross-Validation

To ensure that your model can handle new, unseen data, you need to split your data into training and testing sets. Cross-validation helps you assess the model's performance on yet-seen data. Also, it prevents close alignment with the training data, resulting in inaccuracy when used with live data.

5. Perform Machine Learning Optimization

Fine-tuning your model's settings, known as hyperparameters, is vital to improving its accuracy and efficiency.

Optimization involves adjusting these settings to make the model work better.

6. Deploy the Model

Once your model is well-trained and optimized, it's time to put it to work in a live environment. This is where the model starts performing its intended tasks using accurate data. Containerization is a popular way to deploy models, making updates and scaling easier.

Containerization involves the practice of bundling software code and its associated dependencies into a self-contained entity. This self-contained unit can operate consistently across diverse environments. Within each container, there exists a distinct file system, network interface, memory, and CPU.

This approach ensures a standardized and efficient deployment of software applications across various contexts, promoting reliability and ease of management.

These steps might seem like a lot, but they help ensure that your machine-learning model works effectively and brings value to your organization. However, you should evaluate its performance regularly for improvement.

EVALUATING AND IMPROVING MODEL PERFORMANCE

Evaluating a model is crucial for understanding how well it works in the beginning stages of research and for keeping track of its performance over time. Various tools, known as evaluation metrics, help us determine if our models are performing effectively with new data.

Let's break this down further based on two main types of problems: Classification and Regression.

Binary Classification

In binary classification, where you're trying to predict between two options (yes/no, true/false, etc.), the model often provides a prediction score, which indicates how confident it is about its prediction.

A higher score than the threshold means it predicts one class. But a lower score indicates the other option. It leads to four possibilities:

- True positives
- True negatives
- False positives
- False negatives

Here are the metrics that are helpful in assessing the model's performance:

1. Accuracy: Measures the fraction of correct predictions.

Accuracy = (TP + TN)/(TP + TN + FP + FN) (Kasture, 2020)

Where:

- TP = True Positive
- TN = True Negative
- FP = False Positive
- FN = False Negative

2. Precision: Measures the number of the predicted positive cases that were indeed positive.

Precision = TP/(TP+FP) (Kasture, 2020)

Where:

- TP = True Positive
- FP = False Positive

3. Recall: Measures how many actual positive cases the model predicted as positive.

Sensitivity = TP/(TP + FN) (Kasture, 2020)

Where:

- TP = True Positive
- FN = False Negative

4. Specificity: Measures how well the model predicts the negative cases.

$$\text{Specificity} = TN/(TN + FP) \text{ (Kasture, 2020)}$$

Where:

- TN = True Negative
- FP = False Positive

5. False Positive Rate (FPR): Measures how often the model incorrectly predicts a positive outcome when the result is negative.

$$FPR = FP/(TN + FP) \text{ (Kasture, 2020)}$$

Where:

- TN = True Negative
- FP = False Positive

6. F1 Score: Balances precision and recall.

$$\text{F1 Score} = 2 * TP/(2* TP) + FP + FN \text{ (Kasture, 2020)}$$

Where:

- TP = True Positive
- FP = False Positive
- FN = False Negative

7. ROC Curve: Depicts the trade-off between true and false positive rates.

ROC (Receiver Operating Characteristic) Curves illustrate the balance between two key measures:

- Recall or True Positive Rate (TPR)
- False Positive Rate (FPR)

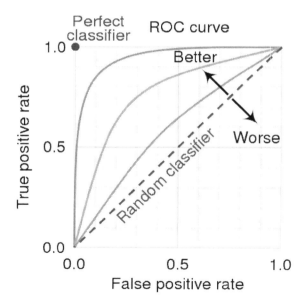

Imagine it as a graph that helps us understand a model's performance. When we calculate TPR and FPR, we're talking about sensitivity and a value derived from specificity.

The ROC curve showcases the connection between a model's ability to identify positive cases correctly and its tendency to classify negative cases as positive wrongly. This balance is essential. Think of it like trying to catch a lot of true positives without mistakenly catching too many false positives.

When we plot the true and false positive rates, it forms the ROC curve. It's like mapping out how well the model can distinguish between different cases. A strong ROC curve closely hugs the upper-left corner of the graph. It is ideal because it means that the model is great at identifying true positives and avoiding false positives.

Remember, a higher Area Under Curve (AUC) in the ROC curve indicates a better model performance. Therefore, finding the right balance between sensitivity and specificity is crucial to creating an effective model.

8. AUC (Area Under the Curve): Measures the model's capability to differentiate between classes.

The AUC metric measures how well a model can give higher scores to positive examples than negative ones. One advantage is that your chosen threshold doesn't influence this measurement. It gives you an overall idea of how well your model predicts without getting into the specifics of a threshold. And if the ROC curve leans toward the top-left corner of the graph, that's a strong indicator that your model is doing a great job.

Multi-Class Classification

In multi-class classification, you don't need a threshold to predict among more than two classes. Instead, you predict the highest-score class. The same metrics as binary classification can be applied here, considering each class's performance.

Regression

In regression, where you're predicting a continuous value (like temperature, price, etc.), you use metrics like Root Mean Square Error (RMSE) to determine the difference between predicted and actual values.

Remember, the choice of metric depends on the issue you're trying to solve. It's essential to pick the metric that aligns with your goals. Evaluating a model helps you understand how well it's doing and if any improvements are needed. Building a great model involves testing and refining it multiple times to achieve the desired accuracy and performance.

In summary, choosing the right tools and libraries is pivotal in the world of Machine Learning, similar to selecting specialized tools for intricate tasks. These choices significantly impact the efficiency and accuracy of model development, shaping the path to success.

Various tools, from TensorFlow and PyTorch to Google Cloud ML Engine and Apache Spark MLlib, offer unique features to streamline the process. Understanding project goals, data analysis, and model evaluation are crucial steps.

Python stands as a versatile language, aiding communication with computers. By making informed decisions and grasping evaluation intricacies, practitioners can craft intelligent computer programs that drive their organization's objectives forward effectively.

Now that you know how to develop a machine learning model, let's discuss which career opportunities will open for you if you have ML skills.

STEPPING UP THE LADDER: CAREER OPPORTUNITIES

A new study from Goldman Sachs has outlined some thought-provoking scenarios regarding the impact of AI on the economy. According to the research, there's a chance that up to two-thirds of jobs in the United States and Europe, about 300 million jobs globally, might be influenced by automation due to advancements in AI (Howard, 2023).

The report also points out that generative AI, an AI that creates content, can take over approximately a quarter of all tasks performed in various jobs. AI can reshape the job market in significant ways.

THE CURRENT JOB MARKET FOR ML PROFESSIONALS

The job market for Machine Learning professionals is shining bright. More and more companies are seeking experts in this field to help them solve complex problems and to make intelligent decisions using data and machines. It means an excellent opportunity for those interested in ML careers. Let's explore some employment trends.

Career Trends in Machine Learning

The demand for ML experts has been growing lately and will keep growing. Here are some critical trends about jobs in Machine Learning:

Good Pay

Machine Learning experts are wanted, so they get paid well. A Machine Learning Engineer in the U.S. can receive an average annual salary of about $152,000 (Glassdoor, 2023).

New Job Openings Due to Machine Learning

Machine learning has opened up many fresh job in the tech field. These roles include software developers, machine learning engineers, data scientists, and AI researchers.

LinkedIn reports that the demand for ML engineers has increased by about 344% since 2015. Also, data science jobs have increased by 256% (Shirsat, 2023). The demand for these professionals will grow as companies invest in machine learning.

Machine Learning-related jobs have surged by almost 75% in the previous four years and will continue to rise (Terra, 2023). Going after a machine learning job is a wise decision for a well-paying career that will be in demand for a long time.

Better Decision-Making with Machine Learning

Machine learning also lets us make better choices in different jobs. Fancy algorithms can spot patterns and scour vast amounts of data that humans might find problematic. It helps companies make decisions based on data, making things work better and earning them more money. Because of this, the need for pros who can understand and explain this data is increasing.

Machine Learning's Impact on Healthcare

In healthcare, machine learning is a game-changer, too. It can look at patient info and discover disease risks, making personalized treatment plans. This feature led to jobs like healthcare data scientists and healthcare analytics pros. Machine learning is bringing significant changes and more chances for employment in many fields.

Industries Hiring Machine Learning Professionals

Data Science and Machine Learning pros are stepping up to help during these challenging times in different sectors.

Healthcare Industry

Right now, the healthcare field needs these experts urgently. They're using data to find solutions for COVID-19. They're studying info from the CDC to discover treatments and to predict how well different drugs might work, making progress faster.

Telecommunications Sector

Companies keeping us connected are dealing with more demands. These experts are using data smarts to solve problems, making sure that we can use tools like video chats. They're even helping improve networks so our online meetings and calls don't get disrupted.

E-Commerce & Grocery Companies

Online shopping is extensive now, and these pros are helping shops handle the surge in orders. They're using machines to move stuff around in warehouses and might even figure out how to send packages using self-driving vehicles.

Financial Industry

Data and ML experts are working with money matters. They're predicting how stocks will do and deciding who should get loans. They're making banking better and quicker, especially for small businesses needing fast help.

Cybersecurity Industry

With more people working online, destructive cyber-attacks are on the rise. These experts are adding smart tools to protect us. They're watching data for strange activity and stopping problems before they get big.

These intelligent people use data and machines to solve tough challenges in each area. Now that you know which industries hire the most ML professionals, let's learn which roles you'll likely take on when you have an ML job.

Roles in Machine Learning Jobs

These roles involve using computers to learn and solve significant problems. In this section, we'll explore jobs like Machine Learning engineers who build innovative models, data scientists who uncover secrets in data, and more.

Machine Learning Engineer

A Machine Learning engineer creates, builds, and uses models that help computers learn things. They work on tasks like teaching computers to recognize images or understand human language. You must be good at programming languages like Python, Java, R, and C++ to do this job. Also, you should know about tools like TensorFlow and PyTorch that help with machine learning. You'll use math and data skills, too. The average pay for this role in the US is about $112,000 annually.

Data Scientist

A data scientist studies big data sets to make predictions and find patterns. They work on determining how customers behave or on finding signs of fraud. This job needs programming skills and knowledge of handling data, statistics, and machine learning tools. A data scientist in the US can receive an average annual salary of around $117,000.

Data Analyst

A data analyst can analyze data to find patterns and trends after careful gathering and processing. They do things like predicting sales or understanding how products perform. To do this job, you need skills in handling data, under-standing statistics, and using tools like Pandas, NumPy, and SciPy. Good communication is essential, too. In the US, a data analyst can receive an average annual pay of about $68,000.

Business Analyst

A business analyst studies how a business works and suggests ways to make it better and more profitable. They look into things like what the market wants and how customers behave. This role requires skills in analyzing, strong communication, knowing about business processes, and skills with data tools. A business analyst can get an average annual salary of around $74,000 in the US.

Machine Learning Researcher

An ML researcher creates new ways for computers to learn. They work on projects like teaching computers to think profoundly or to learn independently. To do this, you must know advanced math and statistics, program well, and be familiar with machine learning tools. The average pay for a Machine Learning researcher in the US is about $129,000 per year (Great Learning, 2023).

These roles show how exciting and diverse machine learning jobs can be. If you're going to be an ML professional, let's discuss the skills you should possess.

ESSENTIAL SKILLS

Let's break down the critical qualifications you need to be a competent ML engineer.

Strong Math Foundation

Mathematics is a powerful tool for Machine Learning. It helps you choose the suitable algorithms, set parameters, and understand statistical models that underlie many ML techniques. Key topics include algebra, probability, statistics, and calculus. Having some grasp of physics concepts can also be a plus.

Computer Basics and Coding

Understanding fundamental computer science concepts is vital. You should know about data structures (like lists and queues), algorithms (methods for solving problems), and their efficiency. You should be comfortable with languages like Python and R for ML tasks, SQL for databases, and tools like Spark and Hadoop for managing large datasets.

Knowing ML Algorithms

You should understand the standard Machine Learning algorithms. They come in three types: supervised (where data guides learning), unsupervised (letting patterns emerge), and reinforced (learning from actions and consequences). Examples include decision trees, regression, clustering, and more.

Grasping Data Modeling and Assessment

Being skilled in data modeling and evaluation is like understanding the language of your data. It's about recognizing hidden patterns and selecting suitable algorithms. Think of it as choosing the best tool for the task, like using a ruler for length or a scale for weight.

Embracing Neural Networks

Neural networks, inspired by our brain's structure, play a significant role in ML. They process data in layers, transforming it for better understanding. Different types exist, like ones for processing text, images, or sequences. Understanding the basics is essential; you can delve into specifics as you progress.

Grappling with Natural Language Processing

Natural Language Processing (NLP) is all about teaching computers human language. It's like showing them how we talk and write. There are special tools, like libraries, to help with this. They break down sentences, find essential parts, and discard unnecessary words. One popular toolkit for this is the Natural Language Toolkit.

Effective Communication

You might not believe it, but good communication is a game-changer. It's about conveying your findings to non-technical people clearly and engagingly. Think of it as storytelling with data. When you share what you've learned, it makes your work truly valuable.

Consider these qualifications as tools in a toolbox. As you practice and learn, you'll get more comfortable using them and combining them to build impressive Machine Learning solutions.

You already know the competencies you need to acquire to be a Machine Learning professional. Let's tackle the career path you'll likely take should you decide to pursue an ML job.

OPPORTUNITIES FOR PROFESSIONAL GROWTH

Exploring Machine Learning can lead to impressive career growth. ML lets you train computers to understand and make intelligent decisions. It is useful in medicine, games, and more. You'll find endless chances to learn, solve problems, and shine in the tech world as you grasp ML's magic.

Machine Learning Engineer

A machine learning engineer uses programming languages like Python, Java, or Scala to run experiments using special libraries for machine learning. In simpler terms, they're like wizards who make sure that the computer programs using machine learning run smoothly and do incredible things. They're the superheroes who ensure that all the technical stuff works perfectly.

Imagine a machine learning engineer who watches all the machines and codes, ensuring that they do their jobs right. They push these machine-learning tools to their limits and even add new tricks. They're like experts who help the rest of the team work faster and better by using innovative computer techniques.

This job is not just for tech companies. Many industries, like finance, healthcare, and even transportation, need these experts to understand vast amounts of data and to find hidden secrets. By doing this, companies become more innovative and better at what they do. As such, between 2015 and 2018, careers for ML engineers grew significantly.

So, how do you become an ML engineer? Here's a path to follow:

1. **Get your college degree:** Start by finishing your bachelor's degree. Good options are degrees related to computer science, math, data science, and more. It's also helpful to study business.
2. **Start with entry-level jobs:** You usually can't jump right into being a machine learning engineer. Begin as a software engineer, data scientist, or something similar.
3. **Get a higher degree:** Most machine learning jobs need more education than a bachelor's degree. Consider acquiring a master's degree in computer science, data science, or something related. Some people even obtain a PhD in machine learning.
4. **Keep learning:** Being a machine learning engineer means that you're constantly learning. Technology keeps growing, so you need to keep up with the

latest AI development. Being a leader and knowing how to manage things is essential, too.

Companies may only need a part-time machine learning engineer. Therefore, freelancing can be a superb option.

Skills You Need:

- Knowing how to program
- Understanding probabilities and statistics
- Figuring out how data works
- Learning about machine learning tricks
- Designing systems

Salary can range from $69,000 to $150,000, depending on your experience.

Data Scientist

Data scientists are like detectives of data. They look at tons of information to find the most critical parts and suggest actions. They spend time exploring, solving problems, and understanding what all the data means, especially with the help of machine learning.

Think of them as a mix of math experts, computer whizzes, and trend discoverers. They're super helpful because they work in both the business and tech worlds. In 2020, being a data scientist was the top job in the US, and the demand keeps growing. Not many people do it, so it can be a well-paying career.

If you prefer to be a data scientist, here's what you should do:

1. **Be familiar with programming:** Learning programming languages is a good idea, even before you start college. Since you'll use them a lot, having a good grip on them is helpful.
2. **Finish your bachelor's degree:** You can study data science, statistics, mathematics, or computer science. You can also go for online programs that help you learn quickly.
3. **Begin with a junior job:** After university, start with a junior role. It helps you learn the ropes and move up the ladder. Junior data analysts or junior data scientists are great starting points.
4. **Go for a master's or PhD:** As in many careers, having more education makes you more valuable. If you study more about data or computer science, it helps. Also, learn about managing data.
5. **Keep learning and working hard:** To get a well-paying data scientist job, put in effort and always keep learning. It helps you get better and move up.

Skills You Need:

- Knowing about statistics and probability
- Understanding math, like algebra and calculus
- Programming skills
- Knowing how to handle databases
- Learning about machine learning and deep learning
- Making data look good with visualization

The salary can be anywhere from $87,000 to $150,000 or even more, depending on your experience.

Human-Centered Machine Learning Designer

The job title Human-Centered Machine Learning Designer might sound complex, but it's not as hard to understand as it seems. These designers create systems that help machines understand things like humans do.

Instead of people having to make programs for every new thing, these designers teach machines how to learn and understand human-like knowledge.

You can find the work of these designers in places like Netflix, where the system suggests what you might want to watch next, or on social media, where algorithms decide what to show you. Even banks use it to catch fake transactions. Netflix saved a whopping $1 billion because of its intelligent machine-learning system that gives you suggestions!

To become a human-centered machine learning designer, you can follow a similar path to the other jobs we talked about. Here's how:

1. **Finish your bachelor's degree:** Getting a degree in information technology (IT) or computer science is a big help for this design job.
2. **Learn programming languages:** Understanding languages like Python and SQL (a way to talk to databases) is vital for your work ahead.

Skills You Need:

- Being good at designing for user experience (UX design)
- Knowing about machine learning
- Being able to design systems
- Understanding data well
- Talking and explaining things clearly (communication skills)
- Being good at researching things

Salary can range from $69,000 to $125,000, depending on how much you know and have done.

Computational Linguist

Today, voice recognition has become more prevalent in our gadgets. As such, jobs related to the technology are also in demand. Computer linguists are like teachers for computers. They help computers to understand what people are saying and to improve because computers sometimes make mistakes.

These experts teach computers to recognize speech patterns and even transcribe words into many languages. This job could be fantastic if you like languages, technology, and improving things!

You'll find the work of these computer linguists in places like when you call your bank or the doctor's office and talk to a computer on the phone. They also make technology work for people who can't see and turn talk into text. Famous voice assistants like Siri and Google Translate also use their magic.

You should obtain a college degree if you prefer to be a computational linguist. However, because it's a specialized career, you should also get a master's degree. You should know much about linguistics, studying how language works.

Here's how you can do it:

1. **Finish your college degree:** A degree in math, linguistics, statistics, or computer science is helpful.
2. **Get a master's degree:** If you can, study computational linguistics or any related course, or you can dive deeper into the subjects you studied in college.

3. **Get certified:** You can learn more without returning to school by teaching yourself or by taking online programs.

Skills You Need:

- Knowing about deep and machine learning
- Being good with spelling, grammar, and sentence syntax
- Knowing at least two languages is a bonus
- Understanding how computers process things
- Using math and statistics
- Understanding natural language processing (making computers talk like people)
- Being good at explaining things

Salary can range from $81,000 to $106,000, depending on how much you know and have done.

Software Developer

Software developers are the creators of computer programs. They have the technical knowledge to develop applications or supervise the team creating them. The software they make lets us do all sorts of things on our devices, like playing games, making spreadsheets, watching movies, or even crafting new programs.

Software developer is a rapidly growing job that's in demand for many companies. There will be around 27,500 job openings in Canada for software engineers and designers from 2019 to 2028 (Robinson, 2021), and many young folks are still interested in studying computer science, which is good news.

To experience the world of software development, here's a plan to follow:

1. **Get your bachelor's degree:** Most software developers have computer science degrees and know much about programming.
2. **Join a boot camp:** Programs like Lighthouse Labs' Web Development Program can give you a mentor, a curriculum, and a great learning space to prepare you for a Junior Web Developer job.
3. **Do internships:** It's a great idea to do internships. You'll learn by doing, learn different programming languages, and understand what's new and cool in the tech world.
4. **Keep learning forever:** In tech, things are constantly changing, so you need to keep learning about new software and languages. Since being a software developer is creative, you'll want to stay fresh with your creative ideas.

Skills You Need:

- Knowing about statistics and probability
- Understanding computer science
- Grasping data structures (how organized info is)
- Getting how computers are built (computer architecture)
- Being good at solving problems
- Communicating well

Salary can range from $58,000 to $120,000, depending on how much you know and have done.

If you prefer to become a Machine Learning professional, you can take any of the career paths mentioned. If you want to hone your skills, practice with the following projects.

MACHINE LEARNING PROJECTS YOU CAN USE TO PRACTICE

Embarking on Machine Learning projects for practice is an exciting journey. It's like training your brain to solve puzzles that help computers learn from data. Through hands-on projects, you'll teach computers to predict, classify, and understand the world better.

Rossmann Store Sales Prediction Project

The Rossmann Store Sales Prediction Project is a machine learning project that predicts sales up to six weeks in advance, once it's been given the data (ProjectPro, n.d.). Kaggle produced the project based on a real-world business problem. Rossmann is present in seven European countries with at least 3,000 drug stores.

Store managers are responsible for predicting daily sales for up to 1 ½ months. Factors that influence store sales include:

- Locality
- Seasonality
- Promotions
- School and state holidays
- Competition

However, the accuracy of the results varies because individual managers base their sales predictions on their unique circumstances.

The project aims to forecast a store's sales on a specific day. The root mean square percentage error (RMSPE) serves as the evaluation basis of the model performance.

NLP Chatbot App

A chatbot is a computer application simulating human conversation using voice or text interactions. As a computer science field, Natural Language Processing (NLP) focuses on the interplay between people and devices using natural language. NLP is helpful in understanding, analyzing, and generating human speech.

NLP Chatbot apps use NLP to understand what people are saying so they can respond sensibly (ProjectPro, n.d.). They are helpful for customer service, personal assistants, and more. A Natural Language Toolkit (NLTK) is a Python library capable of semantic reasoning, parsing, stemming, tokenization, and text classification. It is helpful in NLP research and industry applications.

Loan Eligibility Prediction Project

The Loan Eligibility Prediction Project is a machine learning project that predicts whether a person will get their loan approved using some of the applicant's background information, such as their gender, marital status, income, etc. (ProjectPro, n.d.).

Kaggle produced the project from a real-world business problem. The project aims to predict whether a person is eligible for a loan. The accuracy, precision, recall, and F1 score evaluate model performance.

Credit Card Fraud Detection

Credit Card Fraud Detection employs advanced computer programs, often called Machine Learning, to safeguard people from dishonest transactions (ProjectPro, n.d.). These intelligent systems learn from patterns in genuine and fraudulent transactions, becoming skilled at spotting odd behaviors.

When someone tries to misuse a credit card, the ML program quickly recognizes the irregularity and raises a red flag. This protective technique helps prevent fraud, ensuring that people's money is safe.

Customer Churn Prediction

Customer Churn Prediction, done through Machine Learning, is like foreseeing if a friend might stop visiting a favorite place (ProjectPro, n.d.). Computers use past behaviors, like how often they came or if they got discounts, to guess if they might leave. They help businesses keep regulars happy by offering special deals or better services. It's like a crystal ball for companies, helping them know who might leave and why.

In summary, Machine Learning (ML) offers promising career opportunities as demand for experts in this field continues to grow steadily. With the increasing reliance on data-driven decision-making, individuals skilled in understanding and manipulating data are highly sought after.

ML professionals enjoy attractive compensation, with average annual salaries of $152,000 in the US. This trend has spawned diverse job roles, from data scientists to ML engineers, creating a wealth of employment options.

Industries across the board recognize ML's potential for innovation and efficiency, with the healthcare sector benefiting from personalized treatment plans. Strong foundational skills, practice, and a diverse range of roles make ML an exciting field with abundant professional growth opportunities, shaping the future and impacting various industries positively.

So, if you're excited about teaching computers to learn and make intelligent decisions, pursuing a career in Machine Learning could be your ticket to a fulfilling and prosperous future.

BEYOND THE HORIZON: FUTURE TRENDS AND DEVELOPMENTS

As per a Bloomberg analysis, the worldwide AI market will reach an astounding $422.37 billion by 2028, with a remarkable annual growth rate of 39.4% from 2022 (Zion Market Research, 2022). The outlook for AI and ML is bright and shows tremendous growth potential.

Let's look at the emerging trends in machine learning.

EMERGING TRENDS

Machine learning is evolving rapidly, bringing significant transformations to various fields. Emerging trends like explainable AI, reinforcement learning, transfer learning, and more are reshaping how machines understand and interact with the world. These trends promise greater transparency, adaptability, and efficiency, revolutionizing industries and paving the way for more innovative technologies.

Foundation Models

Foundation models, a significant advancement, have gained recent popularity and are expected to remain prominent. These AI tools are trained on extensive data, surpassing regular neural networks in size.

Engineers aim to enhance machine understanding beyond pattern recognition, focusing on knowledge accumulation. Foundation models excel in content creation, summarization, coding, translation, and customer support. GPT-3 and MidJourney are well-known examples.

Foundation models can rapidly adapt and work with unfamiliar data, showcasing remarkable generating abilities. Leading providers include NVIDIA and Open AI.

Multimodal Machine Learning

In tasks like computer vision or understanding language, models usually rely on just one type of information, such as images or text. However, real life involves many senses, like smell, hearing, touch, and taste.

Multimodal machine learning suggests that since people can experience the world in various ways, building models that can understand multiple senses (called modalities) can lead to better results. This AI concept mimics how humans perceive things using multiple senses simultaneously.

Creating a multimodal machine learning model involves combining different kinds of information during training. For instance, matching images with sound and text descriptions can improve recognition. Although it's a relatively new field, many experts believe that developing multimodal machine learning could be crucial for achieving advanced AI.

Transformers

Transformers represent a prominent category of artificial intelligence architecture, specializing in transforming or transducing input data sequences into different sequences. They employ both encoder and decoder components to accomplish this task.

It's worth noting that many foundational AI models are built upon transformer architecture, signifying their widespread utility in various applications. Transformers, often called Seq2Seq models, are especially prevalent in natural language processing tasks, including translation.

Their effectiveness stems from their ability to analyze entire sequences of words holistically, assigning significant weights to individual terms and then generating sentences in a different language, considering these weightings.

Leading solutions for constructing transformer-based pipelines include Hugging Face and Amazon Comprehend.

Embedded Machine Learning

Embedded machine learning, or TinyML, allows machine learning technology to work on different devices.

TinyML benefits appliances, smartphones, laptops, and smart home systems. The growth of Internet of Things (IoT) analytics, where data from IoT devices helps train Machine Learning models, has led to the popularity of embedded machine learning.

This technology is a significant driver for making computer chips, which are more advanced in many devices. Technological progress has rapidly increased the number of transistors on these chips. This trend will likely persist for years, especially with the rise of IoT and robotics.

Because of this, embedded systems, like TinyML, have become even more critical. However, there are still challenges to overcome, as TinyML needs to be efficient and resource-saving while working well.

Low-Code and No-Code Solutions

Machine learning and AI have significantly impacted almost every area, from banking to farming to marketing. Managers believe that making ML solutions easy for non-technical employees is crucial to keep organizations efficient.

Instead of the expensive and lengthy process of learning programming, it's simpler to use apps that need little to no coding. No-code solutions solve more than just this problem.

Gartner found more demand for high-quality solutions than the capacity to provide them (Moore, 2015). No-code and low-code solutions bridge this gap and meet the demand. These solutions also help tech teams test their ideas faster, cutting development time and costs. Building apps or websites a decade ago needed a whole group, but now, one person can do it quickly.

Around 82% of organizations need help finding and keeping skilled software engineers (Ramel, 2018). They're using no-code and low-code techniques to build and maintain their apps.

While many no-code and low-code options have appeared, they're generally not as good as regular development. Startups that can improve this will succeed in the AI market.

Lastly, cloud computing is vital, especially for large organizations using real-time ML. About 60% of corporate data is in the cloud, which will likely increase (Howarth, 2022). In the next few years, cloud security will get more investment. Gaining resilience to meet the growing ML industry requirements is highly probable.

Federated Learning

Federated learning is a clever way of doing machine learning. It lets many devices work together on a single model without data sharing with a primary server. Instead, each device keeps its data. The central server receives only the updated model parts.

This is very helpful when we worry about our data being private. This means that our data doesn't have to go to one big server for training, which protects it from being leaked. Federated learning also decreases the system's need for computer power and storage because most of the data stays on the devices.

Generative Adversarial Networks

Generative Adversarial Networks (GANs) are a unique computer brain that makes new and real-looking data using existing data. GANs work by making two computer networks compete with each other. One network makes fake data, and the other tries to tell if it's fake.

This trick lets GANs make new data, and it can help make pictures, videos, music, and can even talk like people. GANs are excellent because they can make many different things, allowing other computer brains to learn better.

Explainable AI

Explainable AI (XAI) is a way to make AI more innovative and precise. It helps us understand how computer models learn and decide things. It is essential because we want these decisions to be fair. Regular AI can sometimes be like a mystery box, making it hard to know why it chooses something.

XAI helps us see how decisions are made by showing the crucial factors influencing the choice. It helps us trust AI to make better choices. XAI is excellent for things like money, health, and self-driving cars, where we need to know how they make choices.

Reinforcement Learning

Reinforcement learning is how computers learn by doing things in an environment and getting rewards or punishments. They figure out how to do better based on the results they get. This method has created smart players who win against humans in games like Go and Chess. Robots also use it to learn how to move things and go places.

Transfer Learning

Transfer learning is a method that helps computers get better at one task by using what they learned from a similar activity. For instance, a model that knows how to spot things in pictures could get even better at spotting things in new images by practicing specific examples.

This technique has created outstanding models for understanding images, language, and speech. It's also practical because it can help computers learn with less data in situations without much information.

Now that you know the emerging trends in machine learning, let's discuss its potential advancements.

POTENTIAL ADVANCEMENTS

Machine learning is opening doors for growth and revolutionizing various industries. It helps us make better decisions, offers innovative problem-solving, and delivers information quickly and accurately.

Looking ahead, the future of machine learning is full of exciting possibilities. Its applications cover almost every area, and Natural Language Processing and Computer Vision advances make science fiction real, like facial recognition and self-driving cars.

The next step involves quantum computing, which could transform machine learning using powerful algorithms. It means better data analysis and deeper insights, leading to improved results compared to traditional methods. Big companies are already investing in quantum Machine Learning models, and though they're not ready commercially yet, it won't be long before they are.

We're also heading toward creating multi-use models that simultaneously handle multiple tasks. No more worrying about different frameworks–one model can be trained for various needs.

Moreover, with more data and cloud storage, there's a push for better flexibility in using data across systems. Distributed machine learning will advance, allowing data scientists to integrate their work seamlessly across platforms. Lastly, reinforcement learning will help companies make intelligent decisions in dynamic settings without specific instructions.

Machine learning's future is bright, with innovative advancements that promise to improve our lives and reshape industries. Let's discuss these innovations in detail.

Quantum Machine Learning

Quantum machine learning involves using unique algorithms on devices like quantum computers to boost, speed up, or assist the tasks done by regular machine learning programs. It is also known as quantum-enhanced machine learning. It taps into the remarkable information processing abilities of quantum technology to enhance and accelerate the work carried out by a machine learning model.

While traditional computers have limitations in how much they can store and process, quantum-enabled computers offer a lot more storage and processing power. They can handle vast amounts of information, making them great for analyzing massive datasets that would take regular computers a long time.

As a result, quantum machine learning uses this exceptional processing power to fast-track and improve the creation of machine learning models, neural networks, and other types of artificial intelligence.

Quantum machine learning combines the potential of quantum computing and machine learning to bring about significant changes. Even though it's in its early stages, experts are already searching for ways to use it. These include:

- Creating new algorithms for machine learning
- Accelerating current machine learning algorithms
- Applying quantum-enhanced reinforcement learning, where algorithms learn in a quantum environment
- Creating quantum neural networks that work faster and more efficiently

Although these applications are exciting, machine learning and quantum computing are still evolving. We can expect even more possibilities to emerge in the future.

AI-Optimized Chips

Artificial intelligence is everywhere, integrated into all sorts of computer chips, from tiny ones in IoT devices to big ones in servers and data centers. Industries needing more power will use AI chip technology more. Still, as these chips get cheaper, we'll likely find them in unexpected places, like IoT, where they optimize energy use and other things we might not even realize.

It is an inspiring period for AI chip development. Experts believe that we'll see faster, more advanced processes used because we need better performance. They're also exploring new memory and processor tech types to go with them.

Regarding computer memory, designers are starting to put it close to the computing parts to speed things up. Software drives how hardware is built, with new AI models needing specific chip setups. Fast connections and strong security are essential, too.

In the future, new AI chips might use photonics and multi-die systems to get around bottlenecks. Photonics is a more energy-efficient way to compute, and multi-die systems combine different parts for better performance. One thing is sure: AI chip technology is continuously improving, and companies like Synopsys are helping design better chips for different industries.

IoT Machine Learning

Combining IoT with ML is powerful. It brings more automation, better ways to do things, and more intelligent decision-making to different industries. With all the data from IoT devices and by using special computer programs to understand it (machine learning), companies can learn important things, make intelligent choices, and create new ideas.

This mix of IoT and machine learning can change product design and manufacturing, services delivery, and business operations. It leads to happier customers and smoother operations.

In different fields, we can find many ways IoT and machine learning work together:

- In manufacturing, machines get checked before they break, thanks to machine learning. Sensors in the devices give data, and computers analyze it to know when repairs are needed. It makes work smoother and faster.
- In stores, IoT helps study how customers act. Devices track what they do, and computers look at the data. Then, stores can use this info to make

intelligent marketing plans and to attract more shoppers.

- For farming, IoT measures things like soil wetness and plant growth. Computers learn from this data and say when to water or give fertilizer. They help farmers grow better crops and save resources.

IoT and machine learning offer several advantages: cost savings, improved business efficiency, real-time decision-making, and enhanced data analysis. These benefits are being harnessed across industries and will keep growing with technological advancement.

Big Data

Machine Learning offers efficient and automated tools for collecting, analyzing, and organizing data. When combined with the strengths of cloud computing, it brings flexibility to processing and manages large volumes of data from various sources.

Machine learning algorithms can be helpful in every aspect of working with Big Data, such as breaking down data, studying patterns, and simulating scenarios. All these steps combine to form a complete understanding of Big Data, extracting valuable insights and practices organized for easy understanding.

The connection between ML and Big Data is like an ongoing cycle. The algorithms designed for specific tasks undergo continuous refinement as information flows in and out of the system. This collaboration ensures constant improvement and effectiveness.

The powerful combination of Machine Learning and Big Data drives impressive growth in various industries, with the Automobile Industry being a prime example. In the car sector, merging statistical models with data helps manufacturers figure out how to provide top-notch automation matching users' wants.

Predictive analytics enables manufacturers to keep track of crucial information about vehicle or part problems and share it to the car owners. What's more, modern cars now interact with their owners. They automatically store data about daily routes, locations, and connected entertainment systems. They let users remotely access and manage their vehicles.

THE IMPORTANCE OF CONTINUOUS LEARNING

Continuous learning means constantly gaining new knowledge and skills. It can happen differently, like taking courses or learning from others. It's about wanting to learn and taking on challenges.

Continuously updating what you know or can do is a big help for employees at work and in their personal lives. Here's why it's so beneficial:

- **Being Excellent**: Learning new things boosts how well you do your job and how confident you feel about it.
- **Growing Your Career**: More training, schooling, or skill-building can help you reach your goals if you aim for a specific career or want to switch to a new job.
- **Getting Official**: If you need special licenses or certificates for your job, learning more is necessary.
- **Moving Up and Getting Rewarded**: Putting time into learning can make you better at your job, which could lead to getting promoted or earning more money.
- **Adding to Your Life**: People often have hobbies and interests beyond their jobs. Pursuing those can bring new opportunities and ideas.
- **Being Attractive to Employers**: Keeping up with the latest in your field helps you stay appealing to employers if things change.

So, whether you aim to improve at work or want to grow, learning is the way to go!

RESOURCES FOR MACHINE LEARNING EDUCATION

Machine learning is an exciting and promising field to explore. Whether you're new to ML or have some experience, this section has something for you. So, get comfortable and be ready for an in-depth journey ahead.

Machine Learning Courses

Elements of AI

This machine learning crash course is an excellent resource for anyone curious about how artificial intelligence and machine learning function. It offers clear explanations, numerous examples, and tasks for self-assessment. Whether you're a business owner, marketer, or someone without a technical background, the Elements of AI course tries to captivate your interest.

Check this website:

www.elementsofai.com/eu2019fi

The University of Helsinki developed this course with the Finnish Presidency of the Council of the EU. It aims to provide fundamental ML knowledge for beginners. Its goal is to raise awareness about artificial intelligence on a global scale. You can take the course from its website, elementsofai.com.

Harvard's CS50: Introduction to Artificial Intelligence with Python

David Malan leads the CS50, a popular course at Harvard University. It's available to the public and on EdX. Surprisingly, over a million individuals have watched this course. This significant interest indicates the value it holds.

Go to this website:

www.edx.org/learn/artificial-intelligence/harvard-univer sity-cs50-s-introduction-to-artificial-intelligence-with-python

Malan's unique ability to explain complex concepts that are engaging, enjoyable, and understandable is noteworthy. If you're looking to enhance your technical skills and want to explore machine learning, CS50 is an excellent choice.

Python Programming Tutorials by Socratica

Among the excellent machine learning channels on YouTube, Socratica stands out. Their tutorials on Python programming are nearly as captivating as watching something on Netflix.

Go to this website:

www.youtube.com/watch?v=bY6m6_IIN94&list=PLi01Xo E8jYohWFPpC17Z-wWhPOSuh8Er-

Python is a prevalently used ML and data science program-ming language. It boasts numerous libraries and can serve both backend and frontend programming needs. Utilizing libraries like Tensorflow and scikit-learn, you can quickly begin crafting an AI system. Therefore, learning the fundamentals of Python is a smart choice if you're interested in diving into the world of machine learning.

Google's Machine Learning Crash Course

This course on machine learning using TensorFlow APIs offers a practical way to learn from Google. Even if you have no ML knowledge, this self-study guide can help. However, having basic programming skills and some understanding of math will help you follow along efficiently.

Check out this website:

https://developers.google.com/machine-learning/crash-course

The course consists of video lessons, real-life examples, and interactive tasks. Through these, you'll learn how to code machine-learning algorithms.

ML and Big Data Analytics Course

If you're eager to use ML for practical data analysis, consider enrolling in Big Data: Statistical Inference and Machine Learning. You'll learn the application of ML techniques to real-world data scenarios. You can take the course from futurelearn.com.

Check out this website:

www.futurelearn.com/courses/big-data-machine-learning

You'll become familiar with statistical and machine learning tools like neural networks, decision trees, clustering, and more, which help in dealing with large datasets and extracting insights. You'll also get the chance to practice coding by tackling real-life problems.

To make the most of this course, having a foundational understanding of math and statistics at a university under-graduate level will be beneficial.

Machine Learning Course from Stanford

This course offers a wide-ranging introduction to statistical pattern recognition, data mining, and machine learning. It will teach you how to work with standard machine-learning algorithms and apply effective strategies to solve different problems.

This course includes numerous examples and real-world case studies. These practical examples will demonstrate the potential of ML and AI across various fields. By the end of the course, you'll know how to tackle multiple tasks, from recognizing text to understanding medical information and even creating intelligent robots.

Check out this website:

www.youtube.com/watch?v=jGwO_UgTS7I&amp=&
index=1

While prior programming knowledge is not required, having a solid understanding of mathematics at the level typically attained in a university graduate program is highly recommended.

Machine Learning With Python

IBM offers a Python course that equips you with the skills to create impressive machine-learning programs using this language. Throughout the course, you'll delve into supervised and unsupervised machine learning, uncovering hidden patterns and gaining valuable insights.

Check out this website:

www.edx.org/learn/machine-learning/ibm-machine-learn
ing-with-python-a-practical-introduction

You'll get hands-on experience with popular machine-learning algorithms, such as:

- Classification
- Regression
- Clustering
- Dimensional Reduction

- Widely used models, including Random Forests, Root Mean Squared Error (RMSE), and Train/Test Split

The course is designed around real-life examples, showing firsthand how machine learning shapes our everyday reality.

Machine Learning Books

Machine Learning For Absolute Beginners: A Plain English Introduction by Oliver Theobald

Machine Learning For Absolute Beginners is a beginner-friendly book that comprehensively introduces ML. Despite its introductory nature, the book covers many essential topics, including downloading free datasets, using necessary tools, and understanding machine learning libraries.

Check out this website:

www.amazon.com/Machine-Learning-Absolute-Beginners-Introduction/dp/1549617214

It includes guidance on data cleaning methods, regression analysis, and clustering and even introduces the basics of neural networks. This book is a valuable resource for those looking to begin their journey into machine learning confidently.

Designing Data-Intensive Applications: The Big Ideas Behind Reliable, Scalable, and Maintainable Systems by **Martin Kleppmann**

Preparing data is a crucial initial step that holds the key to your project's success. This book is your guide to effectively organizing your data storage for scalability, consistency, reliability, efficiency, and ease of maintenance.

Check out this website:

www.amazon.com/dp/1449373321/ref=olp-opf-redir

It addresses crucial questions about technologies like message brokers, batch and stream processors, relational databases, and NoSQL data stores. It helps the reader determine which ones suit their needs and shows how they can optimize their usage.

Author Martin Kleppmann thoroughly examines the advantages and limitations of various data processing and storage systems, providing valuable insights into this intricate landscape. Despite evolving software, the core concepts remain constant. With this book's guidance, you'll transform these concepts into actionable strategies, enabling you to fully harness the potential of data in modern applications.

In summary, machine learning is rapidly evolving, with trends like explainable AI, foundation models, multimodal machine learning, and embedded machine learning reshaping various industries.

Foundation models like GPT-3 and MidJourney excel in content creation and adaptability, while multimodal learning mimics human senses for better recognition. Transformers, inspired by human perception, hold potential in advancing AI.

Embedded machine learning brings ML to devices, driven by evolving computer chips. Low-code and no-code solutions make ML accessible, and federated learning enhances privacy. Explainable AI promotes transparency, and reinforcement and transfer learning improve task performance. Quantum machine learning, AI-optimized chips, IoT ML, and big data analytics hold immense potential for the future, promising innovative advancements across industries.

As we've observed, machine learning is a thrilling area with a promising outlook. However, how does this relate to you, the reader? As we conclude our exploration of the ML landscape, let's sum up our journey and consider what it means for those who want to learn, work, or bring fresh ideas to this domain.

CONCLUSION

Machine learning plays a significant role in how current technology functions. It's like teaching computers to learn independently, similarly to how people learn. It helps computers do things like suggesting products when we shop online or helping doctors diagnose illnesses.

Artificial intelligence is teaching machines to be smart like humans. AI is used in many areas like healthcare and transportation, improving our lives. Machine learning has several ways to make things happen. With supervised learning, computers learn from examples. For instance, they can learn to tell if an email is spam or not based on samples we give them.

Machine learning is also about using the right tools. These tools are like unique gadgets that help computers learn better. You can think of these tools as implements similar to what carpenters use to build things. Computers use ML tools to learn. The people who know how to use these tools are in high demand and can make good money.

But don't worry. There are lots of ways to learn about machine learning. You can take courses, watch videos, or read books. You don't need to be a super genius to learn about it. Even if you're in college, you can start learning and exploring this exciting field.

Machine learning is all about data that computers use to learn. The data can be numbers, words, or even pictures. Imagine that you're showing a robot how to identify different animals. You'd show it photos of animals, such as cats and dogs. The robot would use these pictures to learn and better recognize animals.

Data has several types. Numbers are a type of data, like how much something costs. Other data is about categories, like colors or types of cars. There's also data about time, like when things happen. All this data helps computers understand the world better.

Machine learning helps computers make decisions by looking at patterns in the data. It's like playing a game and noticing the rules and strategies. Computers do something similar, but they do it with lots of data.

One crucial thing is to ensure excellent and valuable data. Computers learn the wrong things if the data is messy or inaccurate. So, people who work with machine learning spend time cleaning and organizing the data to ensure accuracy.

Remember, machine learning is all around us. When you use voice assistants like Siri or Alexa, that's machine learning in action. They learn to understand your voice and respond to your commands. When Netflix suggests shows that you might like, that's also machine learning. It learns from what you watch and recommends similar shows.

You can participate in this exciting world, too. You can develop a fantastic idea for a new app or program that uses machine learning. You may find a job where you work with AI and machine education daily.

So, if you're curious and excited about how computers can learn and make intelligent decisions, go ahead and dive into the world of machine learning. An entire world of possibilities waits for you with open arms.

If you've found this book on machine learning insightful and helpful, we invite you to share your thoughts with us and other readers. Your review can provide valuable feedback and inspire others to take this exciting journey of discovery. Your insights matter, and your feedback helps us continuously offer valuable content. We appreciate your involvement in our community of learners!

REFERENCES

AEOLogic. (2022, August 12). *How AI/ML can change the public transportation industry.* AEOLogic. aeologic.com/blog/how-ai-ml-can-change-the-public-transportation-industry

Andersen, T. (2023, March 23). *Why AI requires a new chip architecture.* Synopsys. https://www.synopsys.com/blogs/chip-design/ai-chip-architecture.html

Andreev, I. (2023, June 17). *Continuous learning.* Valamis. https://www.valamis.com/hub/continuous-learning

Ariwala, P. (2023, August 11). *12 ways AI and machine learning are transforming finance.* Maruti Techlabs. https://marutitech.com/ai-and-ml-in-finance/#Future_Prospects_of_Machine_Learning_In

Baheti, P. (2021, August 31). *A simple guide to data preprocessing in machine learning.* V7 Labs. https://www.v7labs.com/blog/data-preprocessing-guide

Bansal, Shubham. (2023, April 20). *Supervised and unsupervised learning.* GeeksforGeeks. www.geeksforgeeks.org/supervised-unsupervised-learning/

Brooks, R. (n.d.). *What is reinforcement learning?* University of York. https://online.york.ac.uk/what-is-reinforcement-learning

CIFDAQ. (2023, May 5). *5 emerging trends in deep learning and AI to watch in 2023.* LinkedIn. www.linkedin.com/pulse/5-emerging-trends-deep-learning-ai-watch-2023-cifdaq

Coursera. (2023a, June 16). *Machine learning in finance: 10 applications and use cases.* Coursera. www.coursera.org/articles/machine-learning-in-finance#

Coursera. (2023b, June 16). *Quantum machine learning: What you need to know.* Coursera. https://www.coursera.org/articles/quantum-machine-learning

Coursera. (2023c, June 16). *What is machine learning in health care? Applications and opportunities.* Coursera. coursera.org/articles/machine-learning-in-health-care

Cprime. (2023). *Five steps to better data quality*. Cprime. https://www.cprime.com/resources/blog/five-steps-to-better-data-quality/

DataFlair. (2023). *5 machine learning case studies to explore the power of technology*. DataFlair. https://data-flair.training/blogs/machine-learning-case-studies/

DataRobot. (2023). *Unsupervised machine learning*. DataRobot. www.datarobot.com/wiki/unsupervised-machine-learning

Davidson, L. (2019, April 30). *The most common machine learning terms, explained*. Springboard. springboard.com/blog/data-science/machine-learning-terminology

DeepAI. (n.d.). *Feature extraction*. DeepAI. https://deepai.org/machine-learning-glossary-and-terms/feature-extraction

Domino. (2021, March 11). *Choosing the right machine learning framework*. Domino Lab. https://domino.ai/blog/choosing-the-right-machine-learning-framework

Edureka. (2023, March 15). *Machine learning and big data: Is it the future?* Edureka. www.edureka.co/blog/machine-learning-and-big-data/#apply

Fayrix. (2019). *10 best use cases of machine learning in finance*. Fayrix. https://fayrix.com/blog/machine-learning-in-finance

Flam, S. (2022, November 1). *Benefits of machine learning in healthcare*. ForeSee Medical. www.foreseemed.com/blog/machine-learning-in-healthcare

Firican, G. (n.d.). *The history of machine learning*. LightsOnData. www.lightsondata.com/the-history-of-machine-learning/

Gavrilova, Y. (2020, April 22). *30 best resources to study machine learning*. Serokell. https://serokell.io/blog/top-resources-to-learn-ml

Gavrilova, Y. (2022, December 7). *Machine learning trends for 2023*. Serokell. https://serokell.io/blog/ai-ml-trends

Gillis, A.S. (2023, July). *Supervised learning*. TechTarget. www.techtarget.com/searchenterpriseai/definition/supervised-learning

Glassdoor. (2023, August 31). *How much does a machine learning engineer make?* Glassdoor. www.glassdoor.com/Salaries/machine-learning-engineer-salary-SRCH_KO0,25.htm

Great Learning. (2023, April 18). *Machine learning and AI job trends in 2023*. Great Learning. www.mygreatlearning.com/blog/machine-learning-and-ai-job-trends/

Great Learning Team. (2023, August 18). *What is machine learning? Defination, Types, Applications, and more*. Great Learning. www. mygreatlearning.com/blog/what-is-machine-learning

Gülen, K. (2023, February 9). *IoT and machine learning: Walking hand in hand towards smarter future*. Dataconomy. https://dataconomy.com/2023/02/09/iot-machine-learning/

Gupta, Mohit. (2023, April 5). *ML: Introduction to data in machine learning*. GeeksforGeeks. www.geeksforgeeks.org/ml-introduction-data-machine-learning

Harkiran78. (2023, February 2). *Top career paths in machine learning*. GeeksforGeeks. www.geeksforgeeks.org/top-career-paths-in-machine-learning/

Harkiran78. (2022, September 5). *7 skills needed to become a machine learning engineer*. GeeksforGeeks. www.geeksforgeeks.org/7-skills-needed-to-become-a-machine-learning-engineer

Howard, B. (2023, April 28). *How A.I. could change the future of work*. CNBC. www.cnbc.com/2023/04/28/how-ai-could-change-the-future-of-work.html

Howarth, J. (2022, November 24). *34 amazing cloud computing stats (2023)*. Exploding Topics. https://explodingtopics.com/blog/cloud-comput ing-stats#top-cloud-computing-stats

Hutchison, G. (2021, September 11). *How to build a machine learning model*. Seldon. www.seldon.io/how-to-build-a-machine-learning-model

IBM. (n.d.-a.). *What is artificial intelligence (AI)?* IBM. www.ibm.com/topics/artificial-intelligence

IBM. (n.d.-b). *What is unsupervised learning?* IBM. www.ibm.com/topics/unsupervised-learning

JavaTPoint. (2021a). *Machine learning life cycle*. JavaTPoint. www.javat point.com/machine-learning-life-cycle

JavaTPoint. (2021b). *Machine learning tools*. JavaTPoint. www.javatpoint. com/machine-learning-tools

JavaTPoint. (2021c). *Unsupervised machine learning*. JavaTPoint. www.javat point.com/unsupervised-machine-learning

Joby, A. (2021, March 3). *What is machine learning and how does it work?* G2. www.g2.com/articles/machine-learning#how-does-machine-learn

ing-work

Joshi, K. (2022, November 11). *5 benefits of using machine learning in finance.* Emeritus. https://emeritus.org/blog/5-benefits-of-using-machine-learning-in-finance/

K, A.V. (2022, February 10). *What are the types of artificial intelligence: Narrow, general, and super AI explained.* Spiceworks. www.spiceworks.com/tech/artificial-intelligence/articles/types-of-ai/#_002

Kapoor, D. (2020, April 10). *Machine learning 101: Essential libraries and tools.* Medium. https://medium.com/analytics-vidhya/machine-learning-101-essential-libraries-and-tools-4ae4b3454586

Karan, V. (2023). *Retail sales prediction.* GitHub. https://github.com/vithika-karan/Retail-Sales-Prediction

Kasture, N. (2020, June 25). *10 essential ways to evaluate machine learning model performance.* Medium. https://medium.com/analytics-vidhya/10-essential-ways-to-evaluate-machine-learning-model-performance-6bf6e11f9502

Kenyon, T. (2021, May 6). *Top 10 sectors for machine learning.* AI Magazine. https://aimagazine.com/top10/top-10-sectors-machine-learning

Khan, J. (2021, May 11). *Data quality challenges when implementing AI.* ITChronicles. https://itchronicles.com/artificial-intelligence/3-data-quality-challenges-when-implementing-ai/

Larkin, Z. (2022, November 16). *General AI vs narrow AI.* Levity. https://levity.ai/blog/general-ai-vs-narrow-ai#

Lynch, S. (2017, March 11). *Andrew Ng: Why AI is the new electricity.* Stanford Business. www.gsb.stanford.edu/insights/andrew-ng-why-ai-new-electricity

Maddali, S. (2021, April 12). *How important is data in machine learning?* Medium. https://medium.com/nerd-for-tech/how-important-is-data-in-machine-learning-259d51e86435

Mayo, M. (2022, May 9). *Machine learning key terms, explained.* KDNuggets. www.kdnuggets.com/2016/05/machine-learning-key-terms-explained.html

Olsen, G. (2020, July 20). *Top industries hiring for machine learning, data science in 2020.* LinkedIn. www.linkedin.com/pulse/top-industries-hiring-machine-learning-data-science-2020-greg-olsen

Pardo, M. (2022, September 22). *Data quality: The better the data, the better the model*. Appen. https://appen.com/blog/data-quality-for-successful-ai-models

Price, D. (2023). *Infographic: How much data is produced every day?* CloudTweaks. https://cloudtweaks.com/2015/03/how-much-data-is-produced-every-day

ProjectPro. (2023a). *Credit card fraud detection as a classification problem.* ProjectPro. www.projectpro.io/project-use-case/credit-card-fraud-detection-classification-problem

ProjectPro. (2023b). *Churn prediction in telecom using machine learning in R.* ProjectPro. www.projectpro.io/project-use-case/forecast-customer-churn-by-building-a-neural-network-in-r

ProjectPro. (2023c). *Loan eligibility prediction project using machine learning on GCP.* ProjectPro. www.projectpro.io/project-use-case/predictive-models-loan-eligibility-classification-sql

ProjectPro. (2023d). *Machine learning project to forecast Rossmann store sales.* ProjectPro. www.projectpro.io/project-use-case/forecast-rossmann-store-sales

ProjectPro. (2023e). *Natural language processing chatbot application using NLTK for text classification.* ProjectPro. www.projectpro.io/project-use-case/nlp-applications-chatbot-nltk-python-example

ProjectPro. (2023, July 15). *Why you should learn machine learning?* ProjectPro. www.projectpro.io/article/why-you-should-learn-machine-learning/362#mcetoc_1fb6n0sudd

Ramel, D. (2018, January 30). *Reports say low-code tools pay off, but many enterprises still unaware.* Application Development Trends. https://adtmag.com/articles/2018/01/30/low-code-surveys.aspx

S., P. (2022, November 16). *How machine learning in healthcare works and why it matters.* Emeritus. https://emeritus.org/blog/ai-ml-machine-learning-in-healthcare/

Schroer, A. (2023, July 27). *Artificial intelligence.* BuiltIn. https://builtin.com/artificial-intelligence

Shirsat, M. (2023, March 21). *The impact of machine learning on the job market: Opportunities and challenges.* LinkedIn. www.linkedin.com/pulse/impact-machine-learning-job-market-opportunities-mithilesh-shirsat

Sidiq, S. (2021, December 5). *Understanding the importance of data for*

machine learning. HackerNoon. https://hackernoon.com/understand
ing-the-importance-of-data-for-machine-learning

Snowflake. (2023). *The role of feature extraction in machine learning.*
Snowflake. www.snowflake.com/guides/feature-extraction-machine-
learning

Sydorenko, I. (2021, May 3). *How to choose the right machine learning algorithm: A pragmatic approach.* LabelYourData. https://labelyourdata.
com/articles/how-to-choose-a-machine-learning-
algorithm#5_simple_steps_to_choose_the_best_machine_learn
ing_algorithm_that_fits_your_ai_project_needs

Synopsys. (2023). *What is reinforcement learning?* Synopsys. https://www.
synopsys.com/ai/what-is-reinforcement-learning.html#3

Terra, J. (2023, August 11). *Artificial intelligence and machine learning job
trends in 2023.* SimpliLearn. www.simplilearn.com/rise-of-ai-and-
machine-learning-job-trends-
article#machine_learning_job_trends_an_increasing_number_of_ca
reer_opportunities

Thomas, M. (2023, February 28). *14 machine learning in healthcare
examples.* Built In. https://builtin.com/artificial-intelligence/machine-
learning-healthcare

YourTechDiet. (2023). *How machine learning will transform transportation?*
YourTechDiet. yourtechdiet.com/blogs/how-machine-learning-will-
transform-transportation

Zabolotnyy, O. (2023). *The future of machine learning.* First Bridge. https://
firstbridge.io/blog/artificial-intelligence/the-future-of-machine-
learning

Zion Market Research. (2022, June 27). *$422.37+ billion global artificial
intelligence (AI) market size likely to grow at 39.4% CAGR during 2022-
2028.* Bloomberg. bloomberg.com/press-releases/2022-06-27/-422-
37-billion-global-artificial-intelligence-ai-market-size-likely-to-
grow-at-39-4-cagr-during-2022-2028-industry

Made in the USA
Columbia, SC
12 October 2023

24371153R00104